THE SUNDAY TIMES
TRAVEL BOOK THREE

THE SUNDAY TIMES
TRAVEL BOOK
THREE

Edited by
RICHARD GIRLING

A GRAHAM TARRANT BOOK

DAVID & CHARLES
Newton Abbot   London   North Pomfret (Vt)

British Library Cataloguing in Publication Data

The Sunday times travel book three.—
  (A Graham Tarrant book).
  1. Voyages and travels—1951–
  I. Girling, Richard
  910.4   G465

ISBN 0-7153-9110-0

Typeset by ABM Typographics Limited, Hull
and printed in Great Britain
by Redwood Burn Limited, Trowbridge, Wilts
for David & Charles Publishers plc
Brunel House   Newton Abbot   Devon

Published in the United States of America
by David & Charles Inc
North Pomfret   Vermont 05053   USA

CONTENTS

EDITOR'S NOTE

This is the third *Sunday Times* Travel Book, and like its predecessors it has involved an unusually large number of people. The fifty pieces collected here were among the many hundreds submitted as entries for the 1986/87 *Sunday Times* Travel Writing Competition. But it is not only to those selected to whom our thanks is due: the enterprise has depended for its success on *all* the writers who entered. Without the stimulus of competition there would be no "best fifty", and no book.

In fact this is not properly the best fifty at all. As in previous years there are a number of richly talented entrants who must count themselves desperately unlucky not to have been included. They have been excluded to avoid duplication of subject matter rather than for any lack of individual merit.

Thanks are due also to *The Sunday Times's* co-sponsors, Speedbird Holidays, and to the judging panel, William Boyd, Dr John Hemming and Virginia McKenna. The three principal competition prizewinners were Julia Butt, for *Les Malheureuses,* Andrew Dinwoodie for *Five Days in Guinea,* and Aideen Mooney for *A Fair Show*.

RICHARD GIRLING
The Sunday Times, London

FENELLA BILLINGTON

A Most Auspicious Star

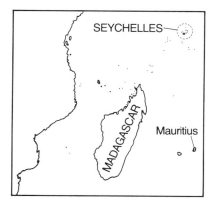

The double doors were stiff with salt from the sea, but I managed to pull them apart and, stepping out on to the beach, gazed at the familiar scene. It was not as I remembered it. The lagoon was oily calm, there was no breeze rustling through the palm trees, the sun had vanished and heavy clouds could be seen gathering on the horizon. There was no-one on the beach.

I felt tired, homesick and dispirited. The journey had been long, but I had been buoyed up with my eagerness to arrive, with excitement at the chance of fulfilling a dream. All I would need during this particular week of March was a clear sky. Now, thanks to the threatening approach of a cyclone named Honoraria, I had to face the sickening disappointment that my dream might not materialise.

From the air the island had seemed like a tiny emerald, nestling in the unfathomable blue of the Indian Ocean. It was all that remained of an extinct volcano and, because of its remoteness from the rest of the world, had housed, and still does, some unique species of animals, plants and birds. The large, slow, flightless dodo had lived here in peace for centuries, for there were no predators on the island. That is, until the advent of Man. Then the story changed for ever . . .

It had been my driver, beaming with pleasure at my arrival, who had first broken the news of the impending cyclone as we drove away from the teeming airport of Plaisance, along the rutted, winding, crowded road that led eventually to the hotel. My heart had given a little lurch. I had known the risk but had thought it was worth taking, for March it had to be. I tried to concentrate on the road, to put dismay out of my mind. It was not difficult. Everywhere one looked there was colour, brilliant in the hot, tropical sun. The Indian women, like butterflies in their dazzling saris, walking with languid grace along the road, waved and smiled as the car passed. So did the children, their deep, dark eyes lighting up with pleasure when I waved back. Luxuriant vegetation abounded, exotic flowers bloomed profusely and the air was hot and scented. It was so beautiful and, at that time, I was so happy to be back.

Later, as I stood alone on the beach outside my room, it was different. The weather had deteriorated alarmingly. Within an hour of my arrival the wind had steadily increased in strength, the palms were lashing their fronds and the rain had begun. Lightly at first, but gradually, through that first evening, the downpour became a liquid wall of water, relentless and torrential as only tropical rain can be.

It was soon impossible to venture into the corridor to walk to the main part of the hotel. I began to feel afraid. Wished I was back home in grey, dull, boring, safe England, instead of seven thousand miles away at the mercy of a force of nature over which there was no control, whose whims were unpredictable and whose reputation was awesome.

Notices were pushed under the doors announcing that Warning Two had been issued and that Warning Three was imminent. This last indicated that the cyclone would hit the island full square in all its fury.

To help pass that endless night, and the long, long day that followed it, I carefully recalled my two previous visits to Mauritius. Then there had been long, lazy days in the hot sunshine, and fun-filled evenings when I had not been alone. Laughter, friends and parties. Happiness and security. Different now. I remembered vividly the places we had visited: the sugar estates, with their romantic names such as Mon Tresor, Belle Vue and Beau Regard; the Pamplemousse Botanical Gardens where there are eighty-seven species of palm, including one specimen unique in the world; the mountainous, jungly Black River region; the bird sanctuary where the fabled pink pigeon is being so carefully nurtured for survival; Ile aux Cerfs, not far away – an idyllic little offshore islet surrounded by limpid turquoise water where one could laze all day in the sunshine . . .

There was a pounding on my door. It was two in the morning. I shot up, heart thumping thickly. A voice called urgently from the corridor, above the din of the storm.

"Missy, Boss say you come quick. Sea coming this way."

Feeling sick with fright, I left. Quickly. I followed the Indian to another room on the opposite side of the hotel on the upper floor. We had to fight our way there, bent double by the force of the wind. There I stayed for a further day, racked with fright and despairing that my once-in-a-lifetime opportunity was disappearing. For I had only one more day and, more to the point, one more night in which to achieve my ambition. After that, the chance would be lost for ever.

There was a book on the table describing the history of Mauritius and tracing its story up to Independence in 1968. It well illustrated the unusual aspects of this small volcanic rock, forty miles long by twenty miles wide, which teems with one-and-a-half million inhabitants. Ninety per cent of them are Indian, but important parts of the mix are the English and French influences that grew up through the historical seesaw as the island changed hands between the two warring nations. It was finally ceded to England after the defeat of Napoleon but was allowed to keep the French language, many place names and the French cuisine. Hence its present day charm, resulting from the successful marriage of three cultures.

As I read on, my desolation threatened to engulf me. My ebb was at its lowest.

As dawn should have been breaking, I suddenly became aware that the buffeting of the wind against the windows seemed to have lessened slightly, that the fury of the palm trees crashing around was abating. I waited and waited, scarcely daring to hope. By seven in the morning I was sure.

Suddenly I heard footsteps running along the passage. They stopped outside my room. Someone banged on the door, calling my name. When I wrenched it open, mind numb with the anticipation of horrors to come, it was the young manager of the hotel who stood there, panting, soaked through, and white-faced with the exhaustion of three nights without sleep.

To my amazement, he hugged me hard.

"Have you heard?" His shout was exultant. "Have you heard? It's changing direction. It's veering right off to the west and going flat out. It's going to miss us completely! It's all over!"

The relief was staggering, weakening. When I could speak, I managed to croak out the question that was uppermost in my mind.

"Is there any chance that the clouds will be gone by tonight? That the sky might be clear? What do you think? Oh, what do you think?"

He considered carefully, knowing only too well how much his answer would mean to me.

"Well, it's possible I suppose. Hard to say. I rather doubt it, I must admit. Cross your fingers."

I did.

During the day that followed I returned to my original room, people began emerging from their hiding places and life slowly came back to the hotel. Late that night, my last before I was due to fly home, I set my alarm for 4am. When it shrilled in my ear I was in a dead sleep and it took me a few seconds to recall why I had woken myself up at such an hour. I remembered.

I tugged open the stiff double doors and stepped cautiously out on to the beach, into total, inky blackness. The night was full of eerie noises. Palm trees crashed all around me, for the wind was still strong, and the sea thundered constantly out on the reef. I stood stock still for a long time, adjusting my eyes to the darkness. I hardly dared look at the sky for fear of what I might see. When I did, my heart pounding, I saw that the cloud had, for the most part, disappeared and that the stars were shining. I strained my eyes hungrily upwards for a glimpse of what I had come so far to see. I looked and looked.

Suddenly, the last thin wisps of cloud parted, and there it was – incredible, unmistakable, unforgettable; the ancient harbinger of doom, a portent, an augur; the cause of wonder and speculation through countless centuries of human observation; the sight that I would one day describe to my grandchildren, as yet unborn, who might, in their lifetime, witness the same. It seemed fuzzy when compared with the sparkling brilliant stars that surrounded it, but its huge tail, streaming away below it, was as spectacular as I had imagined . . .

Halley's Comet . . .

As I gazed and gazed, I wondered how the Earth would be on its next visit, and the next. It seemed benevolent, an object of wonder not fear. Was this the star that Prospero looked upon, as he too stood on a similar island, after a tempest had passed over? Could it have been this same apparition that moved him to say

> *I find my zenith doth depend upon*
> *A most auspicious star, whose influence*
> *If now I court not but omit, my fortunes*
> *Will ever after droop.*

A most auspicious star . . .

I gazed in wonder until the light from the rising sun robbed me of the sight.

Later that same day I flew home to England.

ANGELA SOPER

I Am a Part of
All That I Have Met

Who are these strange women flying from Lima to Arequipa, their legs hidden by canvas gaiters that vanish under cotton skirts? Dancers from Eastern Europe? Missionaries from some chaste sect? Wherever they go, they must attract attention. May they be safe from harm . . .

Every day except Sunday a ramshackle bus goes from Arequipa to the valley of the Rio Colca. Loaded to the axles, it climbs the dirt road to the altiplano, between the volcano El Misti and the snow peak of Chachani. Foreigners are often ill with the altitude but we suffered only from excitement. Where the road crosses the railway to Cuzco a woman got off and plodded to a derelict shanty, weighed down by the baby in her shawl and the bundle in her arms. Later, through windows caked with dust, we saw our first herdsman and his llamas, supercilious animals with coloured ribbons in their ears. A lone vicuña fled like a frightened faun. At last, thirty miles away as the condor flies, through the afternoon storm loomed the bulk of Ampato, the peak we had come to climb.

Nature protects the Colca valley better than most. All round the upper basin at ten thousand feet, rugged mountains rise to twice that height, and downstream the river has cut a gorge which could swallow the Grand Canyon of Colorado three times. In the gorge condors soar and swoop, their cries lost to the torrent. A winding path descends through thousands of feet of columns formed by the cooling of a lava that once dammed the river. On tiers of ancient terraces, the people till the soil with picks, spades, and oxen at the plough, like their Inca ancestors before them.

We camped at dusk in a winter-bare field, separated from its look-alikes by walls of stone and mud, topped with growing cacti. The sun crashed out behind a prickly pear, turning it momentarily into an Inca head-dress, and left us shivering under stars we did not know.

In the morning the children discovered us. The girls wore layers of ragged clothes, jumpers, ponchos, skirts and tracksuits in any order, and sandals made from tyres on their cracked bare feet. Each brown face peeped from under a lacy bonnet with embroidered bands. They let us sketch the designs but would not draw for us. The little boys threw stones at the tents and had to be chased away. They knew exactly how cross we were pretending to be.

Like all the villages, Maca was rebuilt by the Spanish Conquistadors with its streets at right-angles for ease of guarding; no dwelling could have more than one entrance. Eucalyptus trees shade the plaza where, unwittingly, we walked into a fiesta. The villagers gyrated to a brass band – a repetitive dance to a tedious noise – while the home-brewed *chicha* flowed. A woman wearing two embroidered skirts and a garland of fruit dragged me into the dance; she seemed half my height, twice my width, and very strong. I felt confused, vulnerable. No-one was sober enough to give directions, but we escaped to the home of Francisco, who was expecting us. Camped on his field, we were secure.

In Maca the cocks crow at 5am. At six an old bus pulls up at the church and hoots loudly. When he is ready the driver bump-starts it down to the plaza and people with crops for market pile on, their ponchos tightly wrapped against the freezing air. Soon the men march off to their communal work and the sun's rays thaw the stream. Now the women fill their pots and set about feeding children, milking cows, cleaning maize and washing clothes, all in the same water supply. Only Francisco has his own source and a tap. By ten the sun is burning but by afternoon it is imperative to shelter from the wind and all-pervading dust. Peace returns with nightfall and the numbing cold.

Except for Francisco's family, the women would not look at us, but turned away, wishing we had not come. They did not realise that we were women too. We spoke with an anthropologist, a historian, and two medical missionaries, Sister Antonia from America and Sister Sarah from Bombay, who only wished to spend their lives working here. Eventually Francisco found us donkeys and an *arriero* to take our loads up to a training peak.

Away from the village we wore shorts and trainers; our shirts were cached with Francisco and the boots and gaiters went on the donkeys' loads. Tomas, the *arriero*, was a communicative young man. We copied his technique of driving, muttering *"burro, burro"* to the animals, but it failed at the river. They refused to ford the Colca until we unloaded their panniers, so by the time we had dragged the donkeys across and ferried the loads ourselves we were wet, cold and only a mile from Maca. But Tomas pressed on and led us up stony tracks to pitch our tents by torchlight in a place we could not see.

Next day we reached high pastures where great herds of llama and alpaca live on the spiky grass. Our target jutted over the horizon. We camped again at the limit of grazing while Tomas settled among the boulders in his poncho. For him and the burros, a day of rest. The water bottles froze solid inside the tent and delayed our start but soon we came to a hidden lake that mirrored our peak, its surface broken only by diving birds, where we rested on huge clumps of moss which might have been moulded from polystyrene – nothing could have felt less mossy.

Thousands more feet of scree made the altitude tell. Sweets did little for our parched throats as we looked across the Colca valley to Ampato and its satellite peak, which breathed a spiral of gas into the sky. Progress will be easier, we told ourselves naively, when we reach the snow. Alas! We had yet to learn that Andean snow is blown into plates leaning on their sides; it is impossible to walk on or between them. As night approached we packed in, exhausted, below the summit pinnacle of shattered and scary rock and with throbbing heads ran down the screes to relief.

Back at Maca we re-organised for Ampato. Tomas was trusted to load up on his own – a bad mistake. Somehow a loaded donkey set off by itself and could not be found. Tomas panicked – it was his brother's donkey – and we missed ice-axes, sleeping bags and a tent. We split up and roamed the valley, showing everyone a cartoon of the *"burro perdido"*, drafted our insurance claim and offered a reward. Tomas searched desperately; his brother's rage was a terrible thing to see. On the third day of our frustration a *caballero* drove the missing donkey into our makeshift camp in front of his horse. We had lost nothing – except precious time.

So we left the Colca valley to its secrets and trekked towards Ampato. The vastness of the altiplano overwhelmed us and we had little to say. There were animal tracks in all directions. Water was scarce and unpredictable. We passed a shrine to the Virgin Mary, decorated with dead flowers. The nights were bitter and very long; once we seemed to hear pan-pipes. Like the Incas we became sun-worshippers. A woman appeared from nowhere with only a dog, a baby and a toddler, the inevitable coca leaf on her lower lip – the mother, she told us proudly, of eight children. At last we reached the great lava flow that gushed from Ampato ten thousand years ago and spread for six miles. It could have formed yesterday, this vast tongue of cracked and reddened rocks. In a weird landscape we made our base; Tomas turned homewards and we were alone.

We knew already that the enemy had defeated us: we could not climb to twenty-one thousand feet on our last day. But we set off early towards the snow and the smoking vent. Sinking into the ash at each step we managed a mile an hour for six hours until loose boulders slowed us even more. Only extremes of willpower brought us to the snowy col, two thousand feet short of the summit. Cursing the runaway donkey we began the long trek home . . .

Who are these women with chapped hands writing their diaries by the road to Arequipa? Two children of the altiplano come to find out; they are not afraid. The women, in need of human company, share the last few sweets, and make friends. A diary falls unnoticed on the ground, open at words that are not the owner's: "I am a part of all that I have met".

Women cleaning maize at Maca in Peru. (*I Am a Part of All That I Have Met*)

Refilling the radiator before fording the stream. *(Five Days in Guinea)*

Camp life at the Ballinasloe fair. *(A Fair Show)*

ANDREW DINWOODIE

FIVE DAYS IN GUINEA

DAY 1

During the night the rats stole my soap. A garrison of them lived beneath the floorboards and above the sagging, mildewed ceiling of my room. They swaggered about the place as though they owned it – which I suppose they did really: few people must have stayed in the old barrack-house since Nova Lamego was a beleaguered outpost of the Portuguese empire in Africa, surrounded by guerrilla-held bush, as the long war of liberation surged back and forth across the frontier with its neurotic Marxist neighbour, the People's Republic of Guinea.

I rubbed the sleep of history from my eyes and stepped outside into the present: nowadays Nova Lamego is the peaceful market town of Gabu, in the east of independent Guinea-Bissau, and a couple of battered old civilian vehicles wheeze across that frontier each week.

Blinking in the unwashed light of dawn, I located the formidable old Russian lorry that came close to my idea of the archetypal truck. It had one headlight missing and was blind in the other; sported a complete set of bald tyres, and was incontinent on all counts: punctured exhaust, cracked radiator, and oozing a fuse of oil and petrol whenever it moved – which wasn't for some time, as it took all morning to attract a full cargo of thirty passengers and their belongings.

I passed the torrid morning chatting with Hamidou Baldé, an elegantly-robed Guinean who had been working as an "agricultural agent" in Senegal. His ambition was to study at a school he'd heard of for private detectives in Brussels – apparently the best in the world. Hercule Poirot crossed my mind, but Hamidou wasn't looking for a new career: rather, he thought it was essential "to be aware of their methods in this modern world". There were many shadows still in Guinea, which until the revolution two years ago had supported a whole social class of professional informers.

Hamidou's wife sat apart from him throughout the long journey to come, and on the shady verandah of the shop where we waited in the market place. They rarely spoke, but shared the care of their small daughter and occasionally shy, warm smiles. We drank *kankolibá*, a local infusion of stewed whole leaves, which they referred to as "coffee" for my convenience.

I discovered I was at some geo-economic nodal point where the blackmarket values of three currencies coincided:

1 Guinea-Bisau Peso = 1 Guinean Syli = 1 CFA Franc (= 0.2p).

The CFA Franc is one of the sanest things about travelling in West Africa. It's used in a dozen or more states throughout the continent, is convertible as it's tied to the French franc, and is a blessed relief from the perpetual casino of *marché noir* that prevails in most other countries. The ride to somewhere off the bottom of my map cost 1,500 of whatever I chose to pay in.

As I had arrived first I could claim a place in the cab, which can often be worth a five-hour wait: finally, at high noon, the laden truck lumbered out of Gabu. It managed a majestic 25kph in top gear. After an hour of rapid progress we turned off the tarmac and things got slower.

In the midday sun at the empty town of Pitché the mean men of the Guinea-Bissau customs went to work: *"Descendez tous les bagages!"* A lone cyclist and his kitbag were scrupulously searched ahead of us. They took twenty minutes over him alone, but detective Hamidou had deduced his real game, and we imagined him riding away sniggering, pedalling a smuggled cycle across the border and returning by truck each week.

Then the half-dozen officers, most of them wearing sinister Samuel Kanyon Doe-style sunglasses, turned their attentions to the rest of us, and waded through our scattered belongings like bargain-hunters at a jumble sale. They confiscated a few items of interest or value from un-protesting passengers, and collected the customary service charge from the driver.

Everything reloaded, we followed an inconspicuous track south. The lorry's engine laboured heartily. It felt like you could depend on that engine, however much the rest of the vehicle might leak and let you down, though all the gears except fourth seemed to grind their teeth sadistically against mine.

When secluded by a clump of trees, we heaved to a halt in a cloud of our own dust, whereupon most of the men leapt out and thrust bundles of CFA banknotes at the *chauffeur*. Trial and expensive error seemed to have shown this to be the safest strategy for entering Guinea with hard currency, as the Customs search very thoroughly and con-fiscate all *dévises*: the driver is the only person by custom never searched, since he has to carry assorted currencies to ply his trade, and anyway gives the *douaniers* good *argent de passage*.

The *chauffeur* collected the fistfuls of cash and issued carefully-worded duplicate receipts on scraps of paper, an elaborate transaction as most of the men seemed to be called Mamadou, Diallo, or in several cases both – the driver himself, for one. I reluctantly handed over a sealed envelope of French and CFA francs, sterling and dollars, and kept the pesos, dalasis and traveller's cheques to fend for themselves. I wondered whether it might have been a better bet to conceal it all somewhere in the truck, until I saw later how assiduously that was searched. The Mamadou Diallo we were entrusting our collective fortune to was a shrewd, stringly fellow in a thin safari suit: all his buttoned pockets now bulged extravagantly.

During this flurry of financial fervour the women sat calmly in the back of the truck and chatted over their sleeping and suckling babies, having concealed their money with the minimum of fuss.

At the border river a final fastidious Guinea-Bissauen official inscribed comprehensive details of identity cards and passports in a huge, historic, hidebound Portuguese ledger.

I sat in the shade of a Koliba tree until the rubber-stamping was finished. Then the broken cable-raft – which had once possessed the useful facility of a working winch – had to be tugged back from the Guinea bank 200 metres away across the tree-lined Kolibar River. The *bac* arrived bearing an irate, almost-naked old woman and three half-washed great-grandchildren she had lately been lathering in another country. They all leapt soapy and shrieking from the raft as the truck growled up the ramp. Most of the men gallantly hauled on the hawser to propel us across, while the Women's Institute assessed our efforts amongst themselves.

Up the steep bank on the Guinean side there was a cosy collection of wood, cane and thatched huts, warm and welcoming in the afternoon sunlight. The gendarmes harassed the other passengers while the commandant and his wife invited me to share their bowl of rice, vegetables and meat. When we'd finished I asked what we'd eaten, and he thoughtfully fetched the cute little bush-antelope's head in case I'd like a souvenir.

He demonstrated his juggling skill with four green oranges while he told me how much freer Guinea now was under the Second Republic: since his death, the tyrant Sekou Touré is seldom mentioned by name, but referred to obliquely as *"l'ancien régime"* or *"la République Populaire"* (with heavy sarcasm).

There were rigorous baggage, body and vehicle searches going on all around, but the commandant waved his men past my pack. He detailed one of the soldiers to take his prized Italian hunting-rifle – which had recently dispatched Bambi – and ride shotgun with us to the next village to fetch him his blue suit, a razor and any edible wildlife he came across on the way.

"Hey, *chauffeur!*" he called, "Did we remember to search you too?" Mamadou grinned conspiratorially and went on attending to his engine. His apprentice emerged from under the chassis – where he had been variously drenched while failing to staunch the flows from the broken radiator, oil leak and ruptured fuel pipe – and lit an heroic cigarette.

The track was rougher on this side of the river, and it was almost dark when we stopped for the night at the village of Foula Mori. There were more immigration formalities by the light of a kerosene wick in a beer bottle, which gleamed on the gendarme's cap badge and buttons as he stamped documents and entered particulars on sheets of graph paper torn from a child's exercise-book covered with Disney cartoon characters.

Beside a log fire, beneath a tree as tall as a cathedral, some of the village woman brought me a mat, blankets and pillows, and *kankolibá* in an old oil-can – probably a relic of one of Mamadou Diallo's previous transits.

As I fell asleep, someone strummed a *kora,* a transistor radio was announcing an astronomical devaluation of the Syli, and Orion straddled the heavens.

AIDEEN MOONEY

A Fair Show

Through Leinster and Munster, along Connaught lanes and highways there's a movement. Brazenly on verges, tucked behind hedges, parked in laybys there are caravans. Not tourists but the homes of the Irish Travellers, the Tinkers. Herds of their horses hold up the traffic. Greys, chestnuts, roans, bays and the especial pride, the batty mares: great coloured, patched horses, piebald and skewbald, hooves swathed in shaggy hair. They're all heading along roads which lead to the nub, the October fair, Ballinasloe. A convergence for horses and horsemanship, dealing and drinking, exchanging news and the "crack". "You'll never see as many horses together as you will at Ballinasloe. Once Seamus McGinty rode down the high street at the head of sixty, his sons as outriders flanking their wealth."

Beating hooves on the smooth tarmac. Sealed in our motor car we've drawn up behind a berserk cacophony of colour – buttercup, marigold, poppy, cornflower, peagreen and fuchsia burst out of the drear drizzle. A barrel top, horse-drawn waggon. Polished brasswork and picture panels of horses and dogs lurch and sway on their way. The grey-haired wife expertly handles the flat cart at a sharp trot.

"Charlie Donovan! I remember when I first met him. A wagon hurtling down the hill towards me. Out of control. Driverless? But when it was almost on top of me I saw a pair of boots on the footboard and then the rest of Charlie, flat on his back, reins in one hand, whip in the other, shouting the horse on. Dead drunk, laughing and roaring, off on a bender. Two miles behind was his wife, sedately on the flat cart piled high with their breakables, smiling, letting him have his fling."

Motoring down to the pub that evening, and there, in the gentle rain, beside the road, is his camp. The old man with his pipe squats by the fire. A blackened kettle hangs over the flames from an angled rod stuck into the ground. A chicken is tethered to a wheel of the cart by a piece of string knotted around its leg. A litter of terrier pups in a cardboard box. There is nothing modern, nothing plastic here. He sees no point in change, everything as it was, always has been. His wife's inside the waggon on the high back bunk. I get a glimpse when I greet her, the roof's lined with a patterned cotton fabric and a small wood-burning Queenie stove gives off a good heat. I'm catching the last moments of an era, sharing their fire, listening to the stories of an old-time traveller. "There was wance upon a time, and a very good time it was. Neither my time nor your time but somebody's time . . . " Embers fall, gold-vermillion. We accept a cup of heavily sugared tea. "Yes we'll be at the fair."

It was on the next day that we stood on the hill looking down on the crush. Sleek flanks, arched necks, powerful hindquarters, glossy and firm flesh. Whinnying and snorting; stamping hooves. I want to bury my head in a mane and remember childhood adventures of riding lessons. Horse and candyfloss in the breeze.

On the fairground there is a sharp division. One half is farmers and county. Fine-boned hunters with fine-boned riders in tight, white jodhpurs and long, black boots. Arrogant and upright on their proud animals; tight, white control. On the other side are the Traveller horses. "You'll never see a saddle at a Traveller fair." The young lads are equally as proud of their horsemanship. A slap on the arse, shouts of encouragement and the horse plunges through the crowd, a wave of people backing off before it. It's a matter of balance. They sit well back, tipped on the base of the spine, reins held high, legs loose. It's so easy, flowing with the horse in a mad hurtle, this is the way Travellers ride. Up down, up down, this is the way the Gentlemen ride.

The Travellers give a spirited display. That horse has good brakes! It stops short in a controlled skid, heads again into the crowd and pulls up two feet before a wall. Some pull light sulky traps, merely a tubular steel frame, and there are some alacritous and alarming turns in small spaces. The horse rears. There are people under the flailing legs. Hooves hit the ground and it races back. In the crowd, watching the show, keen eyes detect almost imperceptible faults. Heavy, dark tweed suits and intent, rough-hewn faces. They sweep you out of the way before a torrent of horse but you sense they'd get a thrill from any catastrophe. You creep behind the lines of tethered animals. Is that hoof cocked to kick?

A deal is being done over a dog. It hinges on the middleman. He's brought buyer and seller together and now steps into the spotlight nudging the punter up a few pounds, drawing the asking price down. The audience clusters closer, watching one intransigent face and then the other. Voluble, cajoling, seducing, the moving force of the negoti-ation, this middleman will persist until the deal is done. The asking price was a hundred pounds. Now there is stalemate at fifty and eighty. Notes emerge. Cash is pushed into the owner's hand. "Now that's all he has except for five pounds for petrol home." The lure of a handful of paper. Will he? There's a nod and a smile and the dog is passed over with one pound for change "for luck"; in accepting money you must always return some. A spit into the palm and a thwack of hands and the deal is ratified. The middleman relinquishes his role and relaxed, happy murmurs discuss the dog's heritage and abilities. The crowd smiles with genuine delight that a deal has been done.

Lips dip into foaming white and take deep draughts of black:

"You remember that mare I bought in the spring? She'll fetch a good price now. I knew she had the makings. For sure, that meadow she was in, she hadn't room to change her mind."

And, "I'm telling ye, brush the animal with sump oil and that'll keep the flies away".

By late afternoon, seeping from overflowing pubs, the men are at the height of inebriation. Growls of aggression rumble in corners. Every man has a stick. Trying to herd animals into a horsebox a dozen Travellers have created a frenzy of disorder. The creatures are taking a thrashing from the ash plants, hazel wands and lengths of plastic tubing. Then in a flash the herd have dashed free of the cordon of men. Fuel for mercurial rage. Explosion. Each man has turned upon his neighbour. Bash, thrash, wallop. Comic strip figures. Little dancing men from *Beano's* pages. An old character, watching, catches one of the animals by the head, steadies it, whispers in its ear, strokes its nose and the horse is calm. That's a fellow with a genuine understanding and communication with horses. He'd know all the old cures.

The cures, the stories, the old nomadic way of life. How soon until it's all lost? There are some people who are fanning the embers of this dying fire. They came over to Ireland as hippies in the sixties, seeking waggons to live out gypsy dreams. The Tinkers thought they were of one travelling family. On Irish roads there were the tribes each with their chief, the Danahas, McGinleys, Donovans, Connors, Clarkes . . . and now the Hippies. Many of the Irish Travellers adopted their long hairstyle, and hippies were respected for their dealing abilities and that they bred fine hunting dogs. Traveller girls lived with hippy men, and Tinker men lived in greedy expectation that they might share some of the hippy women who moved so easily from partner to partner.

Now the hippy waggons ring the campfire. Their shafts point inwards and become the spokes of a giant wheel with the fire as the hub. The hub of camp life. There's always a kettle on the boil, someone chopping vegetables for the pot. Take a place beside the fire and become part of the circle, the chat, the stories. In a circle we are strong. But this camp is only a pretty, antique button lost in a plethora of plastic and aluminium Traveller caravans. Some are lived in and some seem to be only for show. Strips of glittering chrome on the outside and lines of shining cooking pots and china inside. Pots and china reflected a thousand times, bedazzling in an interior panelled with mirrors.

A glowing fire is the only gleam amongst the muddy and soot-encrusted hippy utensils. Last night there was some unpleasant communication between the women of the two camps. An English girl, just over, some said she'd just been flirting, some a gang-bang with the Traveller men. Whatever, she'd broken a living code amongst the women, and to be fair, they came to warn her friends "get her out of here or she'll find a knife in her back". She went.

We went. It was raining and our windscreen wipers had been stolen.

KATHERINE HEDGES

Pat Phoenix Died Today

"At Wimereux in August there is a Mussels Festival with flowered float parade and seafood tasting."

All the way over to Boulogne my son regaled me with snippets from the handouts they gave us at Folkstone. I scanned the coastline for Wimereux but all I saw for miles were topless sunbathers. I'll never have the nerve. Who wants burnt nipples anyway?

An Eastender with a ghetto-blaster swung the news at us as he patrolled the deck.

"Pat Phoenix, who is suffering from lung cancer, had a comfortable night."

People paid little attention to this as our ferry, *Hengist,* was negotiating the entrance to the harbour.

"Who was Hengist?" I asked my son.

"First King of Kent, invited by Vortigern to defend Britain," replied Matthew.

He packed his handouts away and put forward our watches.

Boulogne-sur-Mer! A 2CV buzzed by like a liver and cream wasp. A *boulanger* van honked dementedly after it. On the Quai Gambetta a courier in a red and white blazer waved a clipboard, gathering his flock for a coach trip, perhaps along the coast or for *shopportunités* at the Auchan hypermarket. His rosy cheeks, hooked nose and striped jacket lent him an air of Punch in a rare convivial mood.

The Orient Express was waiting too, a bit standoffishly, to receive its customers from England. Such ornate livery! Black and crimson and gold, it was very regal, rather like a packet of luxury Russian cigarettes laid out end to end.

"Like a cardboard model of itself," said Matthew.

Though very inviting, the restaurants were too dear for us so we looked for Place Dalton and its open market. Here we got baguettes, two slabs of runny Brie and mammoth Marmande tomatoes. Orange cans of Fanta and misty green bottles of beer *sans alcool* completed our feast. A man who sold nothing but biscuits pressed two broken custard-creams into our hands. They had layers of yellow and pink filling and left a sickly taste, a bit like dolly-mixtures.

We lugged our provisions up to the *haute ville,* which is the old medieval area of Boulogne. Virtually all the ships that lie within the ramparts here line the rue de Lille. At Nicholas and at Vins de France there were remarkable bargains, but we didn't avail ourselves. We stood in silence at Confiserie Bethouart where there was a ravishing window full of marzipan fruits and fish. It might have been a set for Hansel and Gretel – pineapples, pears, lush snails, herrings, seafoods, shells, even tins crammed with silvery marzipan sardines.

Though it was sunny, the streets around here were all but deserted. At the corner of rue de Lille we saw an old woman in a calico nightie, feeding pigeons at a ledge. She stood at an oriel window, crumbling yesterday's bread. Her expression was something to see as the birds came to rest on her gnarled hands. She started when she saw us and her birds vanished. I thought of Flaubert's *Félicité* and her *perroquet gigantesque.*

The medieval ramparts form a rectangle which encloses the *haute ville.* By the shallow steps here, well shaded by a horse-chestnut, sat a young mother. In one hand she held her magazine, *Marie-Claire,* and with the other she rocked her baby's pram lightly over the first fallen conkers on the gravel. Bent so attentively over what she was reading, she had the concentration and the stillness of a genre painting. The baby, far too plump for its pram, was smooth and shiny as a new croissant. On the bib of its rompers was its name – Hervé.

The ramparts contain seventeen towers and four gates. We lunched at *tour verte.* It was after twelve, a mild warm late summer day. On the lawn a few yards away a circle of nuns sat mending linen. One of them was reading to the others. Shrubs, sheltered by the sunny ramparts, blazed with blossoms – purple, violet, lavender blue. We rubbed bits in our hands to get the scent. It was peculiar, a lemony smell. Below us the town, the harbour and the vast calm channel stretched out peacefully.

"Julius Caesar used this area as a base for his invasion of Britain," Matthew informed me, swigging his beer *sans alcool.*

The ghetto-blaster fiend came puffing up to the *tour verte,* laden with iron saucepans, sets of crystal glasses and carrier-bags of duty-free, clearly tuned in still to the BBC.

"Children in Manchester are saying prayers today for Pat Phoenix. Her husband maintains a constant vigil at her bedside."

Evidently the news meant nothing to the nuns, though their eyes followed the noise reprovingly.

"Let's go and look at the Cathedral, Matt." The Cathédrale Notre-

Dame has a marble altar and a fine italianate dome. It was too cool for us inside but the spicy incense and the candles were seductive. We never got to see the recommended Norman Crypt, as they were about to start mass.

"Any idea where the toilets are?"

"Place Dalton and rue Nationale."

I went in some nettles behind the Cathedral as somebody went whistling by on the ramparts. I prayed he wouldn't look down.

The modern area of Boulogne, the *basse ville,* has largely been rebuilt after damage from Allied bombs. At Fromagerie Philippe Olivier we goggled at two hundred cheeses before coming away with a crusty triangle of Camembert, succulently steeped in local *calvados.* I ached in Nouvelles Galeries after two fine mannered figurines, evocative of *Les Enfants du Paradis.* One was a soubrette, pert and engaging as Garance, and the other a harlequin, naif and mournful as Baptiste. Though we lacked the nerve to enter Parfumerie Gilliocq, my son fixed me for ever in Polaroid there, before its glitzy pink façade.

"You said we could go to the mini-golf."

"You're the guide."

Beyond the harbour lay the little park where *les chiens doivent être tenus en laisse.* Sure enough, on the whole, they were. The mini-golf course was a model of the *haute ville* – castles, turrets, gables, lodges, a medieval landscape in miniature. Cedars and scented pines fringed this sandy area of the park. It was fresh and pleasant. Playing behind us on the course were an elderly French couple, reticent and watchful, like figurines in the shadowy corner of a Monet garden.

Once I hit the ball right over a turret and into the park. A terrier, not *en laisse,* ran up and chewed it.

"*C'est difficile n'est-ce-pas?*" said the old lady.

"You wally," said my son.

Refreshed by *citron pressé* we lingered in the park, at a café table, looking out to sea. In the late afternoon the harbour was smellier – stagnant water, fish, drains, diesel. A crane and a grain-elevator, angular and neat as Meccano, clanked away on the quai, while *la Liane,* a rusty grab-dredger, lunged tenaciously at the silty mud in the harbour.

Our ferry appeared far off, like a bath toy becalmed on the horizon. We made out the Union Jack, and later HORSA, LONDON.

"Horsa, brother of Hengist was eventually killed in battle."

The blue and yellow funnel was a squashed liquorice allsort, stamped into the deck by some giant.

"I am the salt of the earth," said Horsa, throbbing importantly towards Boulogne.

Longer shadows darkened our road back. On the side of a grain warehouse we passed a poster of a cat of Cyclopean proportions. It had elongated droopy whiskers and sad, sad eyes, round and green as gooseberries.

"Ce soir y'a pas de Kit-e-kat," it complained hungrily.

A necklace of *frites* vans graced the Quai Gambetta now, anticipating the homeward–bound. We took away two newspaper cones full, splashing them with fruity brown sauce.

The final van sold peasanty soup bowls painted with yachts and sea-gulls. Names encircled the rims. I found *Cathérine* at once, but we had to dig deep for *Matthieu*.

"Why did you call me Matthew?"

"When you were inside me I followed *Roads to Freedom*. On BBC 2. I was nuts about Matthieu."

The bowls, meticulously wrapped for us in layers of flower-patterned tissue paper, saw the last of our francs.

The cliffs between Folkestone and Dover held on to the late sun. One by one watches were put back and last glasses of draught Stella balanced on the rails as people congregated for the arrival. As he swung the ghetto–blaster near us one last time, I saw how the French sun had reddened the back of his neck.

"Pat Phoenix, star for many years of the serial *Coronation Street,* died today in a Manchester hospital. The end came peacefully. Her husband was at her side."

"She was a real scorcher," he said.

"A belter," agreed Mr. Punch, blowing his hooked nose.

JERRY CALLOW

THE CRAZY KUMBH

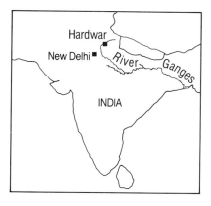

It is the largest gathering of people in the world, it happens every twelve years and it could happen only in India. They come by train, they come by bus, they come on foot. But they come. They come to bathe in the Holy Mother Ganga. This year four million come to be in one place at one time. The place is Hardwar, the time is eight minutes past two on the morning of April 14th, 1986. It is unbelievable. It is unique. It is the great Kumbh Mela.

The Hindus love a good legend and the mythological beginnings of this unparalleled religious spectacle are no exception. Many moons ago, the son of Indra, king of the Gods, managed to retrieve (not unlike some sort of celestial "Repo Man") a *kumbh* (pitcher) filled with the elixir of immortality that some demons had stolen from the bottom of the ocean. During the twelve-year chase that followed, one of the places in which he and his ambrosia happened to take refuge was Hardwar. Meanwhile . . . back on earth it seems the Mela started as a vehicle for the propagation of Hinduism; a forum where the Sadhus, the Holy Men, could wax enthusiastic about its many virtues to all who cared to listen. That wasn't very many, so, in order to attract more people, it was decided that anyone who bathed in the Ganga at a Kumbh Mela would be absolved of all their sins. No questions asked. This, of course, had the desired effect, and since the thirteenth century it has become part of Hindu culture.

This year there had been a call for the Mela, once again, to be the platform for a serious Hindu revival, but the millions flooding into Hardwar didn't care. They were coming because of their unquestioned belief that bathing in the Ganges on April 14th would cleanse their souls; the Holy River washing away those stubborn sins and taking them, and any other flotsam that might happen to be in the water, somewhere off in the direction of the Bay of Bengal.

To wash my own sins away, even at such an auspicious occasion, would have taken far too long, so, leaving my swimming trunks in downtown Delhi, I found myself sitting on the top of a crowded pilgrim bus heading for Hardwar in the foothills of the Himalayas. Jupiter was in conjunction with Aquarius and, as any astrologer worth his star charts should know, it could mean only one thing. After two months of frenzied build-up, the next day would be the climax of the Kumbh Mela. Four million sinful Indians all trying to bathe in the same place at the same time? There was only one place to be in India and, excited and nervous, it was exactly where I was going. Nothing could have prepared me for the next twenty-four hours.

From several kilometres outside the town a seething mass of humanity was inching its way towards the banks of the Ganga. It was on a biblical scale. Only Charlton Heston was missing as this swarm of people was sucked inexorably towards the water's edge; the river of Life and Salvation. Gradually, as the streets narrowed, the multitudes became locked together into a solid lump and I was no longer able to stop or go back. It was too late, and as night fell I was pulled deep inside the Kumbh Mela and deep into India.

Lost in a swirling mass of people, colour and energy. Wet, cold, shivering bodies pushing their way through the crowds; people silhouetted in the clouds of dust thrown up into the air; small babies being held up and unceremoniously plunged headlong into the water; old couples desperately clinging to each other and to their precious vials full of "Holy water"; the very old being carried down to the river for their last act of purification; and everywhere people bathing in touching individual displays of faith.

Inevitably Melas such as this also drag the weird, wonderful and absolutely berserk out of the Indian woodwork, and that night they all seemed to have appeared in Hardwar (apart from the infamous and lusty Bhagwan Rajneesh, holed up somewhere in Uruguay). There were the magicians; the Yogis; the jugglers; the preachers; the Hari Krishna devotees (looking more at home if no less limp than they do wandering down Oxford Street); and, perhaps the craziest of all, the Sadhus. Many of these supposed spiritual pioneers of Hinduism were sitting in large groups smoking their *chillums* (pipes) filled with marijuana, which they held high above their heads, and which were no doubt taking these holy men even higher. The Mahatma condemned this sort of hollow spirituality saying, "These men were born only to enjoy the good things in life". However, this couldn't be said about some of the "Naga" Sadhus who, standing near the river, painfully demonstrated their rejection of desire by piercing their penises and hanging rocks from their genitals. This extraordinary self-mutilation didn't even merit a free radio. Maybe they should have kept their lingams in their lunghis?

These colourful characters were a minor distraction compared to the frantic scenes at the water's edge, where people were pouring down the steps into the river and whole families, young and old, were splashing each other in a joyous celebration of their faith. Small fires were burning among the blanket of people that stretched back from the Ganges, and while some slept others were chanting or singing. Occasionally the loud moan of a conch shell summoning the spirits soared above everything. There was nowhere to rest as the crowds moved on and the bathing ghats, stretching up and down both banks, were covered in a solid wave of pilgrims forcing their shaved heads down to the water. It was a humbling experience.

In the middle of the night the crowd thickened, winding its way through the bamboo barricades and over the thin wooden bridges to Hari-Ki-Puri (the holiest site in Hinduism, where the waters supposedly wash away seven generations of sins). The piercing whistles of the police, trying to control the crowd, shrieked above the hum of chanting and prayers, and a sudden surge forward lifted me off my feet. Considering the painfully short time and small space the gods have given the Hindus to attain salvation, the crush was quite understandable.

Among this unimaginable human chaos, pilgrims pushed their way through until they found what space they could; undressed and, impervious to everything and everyone else, lowered themselves privately into the Ganga, offering the Holy water skywards in cupped hands.

For some this was the most important moment of their lives and, as these people immersed themselves in the water and their belief, it was impossible not to feel the power of their faith. This was the heart of the Kumbh Mela. Garlands of yellow marigolds were swallowed up by the water as it rushed past, and flickering spots of light from hundreds of small candles danced all over the human mosaic that dissolved into the river. It was indeed a spectacle for the gods, and wedged into this crucible of believers you could feel the magic in the air.

The splashing, the bathing, this awesome demonstration of faith carried on all night, and it was only as the sun rose that the frenetic activity at the ghats seemed to slow down. The crowds began to line up behind the fences, in the trees, packing the embankments and covering the ground like an enormous, colourful jigsaw. They were waiting for the climactic six-hour procession of the different *akharas* (holy sects), on their way to Hari-Ki-Pari.

News had spread of a stampede early that morning in which fifty people had been crushed to death, but this was India and it had happened before. So, apparently indifferent to the tragedy, thousands of completey naked Sadhus brandishing maces and spears swaggered past with their matted hair, smeared in cow dung, trailing behind them in the dust. Other *babas* waving their huge banners lapped up the adoration of the crowd. It would have been quite easy to seat a family of four on the buttocks of some of the larger gentlemen arrogantly wobbling out in front. After them came their "Spiritual leaders" sit-

ting regally in their brightly decorated chariots, distributing considerable largesse while their emaciated acolytes struggled manfully to stop
these "men of God" toppling earthwards. Had these *sanyassis* really
rejected the pomp and vanity of this world?

   As the crowds cheered and bowed to this impressive, imperious
cavalcade, I looked back towards the Ganga at the unending stream of
pilgrims still bathing in their own private rituals of purification, and I
thought of the old couple huddled together struggling along by the
river with nothing but each other and their faith. What *was* all this?
This was India and India at its best. Crazy, magical, and always
unforgettable.

Part of the main procession at the Kumbh Mela, the largest gathering in the world.
(*The Crazy Kumbh*)

Dressing up and undressing for the Holy Mother Ganga. *(The Crazy Kumbh)*

Following the signs at Mt Hiei, Kyoto. *(Ryokan)*

JANET CLAXTON

RYOKAN

Of course we want to stay in truly genuine Japanese accommodation. No we don't wish to go to the high rise luxury hotels that foreigners usually visit. We're in The Land of the Rising Sun for three months, so let's live like they do. Two months have already passed of life in Japan, cocooned by the Western-style apartment belonging to the university. Plenty of time to get over the culture shock and to accept life in a very different land. Clutching our JNR rail passes, we had departed on a week long, three-thousand-mile train journey. Being government workers, albeit the only Westerners, we'd use their facilities and stay each night in one of their hotels.

The first encounter with something new makes the biggest impression. Ryokan – what a strange word – but this building looks far from strange. Concrete, windows, three floors, quite normal. Let's go in and relax. No-one around – just rows and rows of neatly placed brown plastic slippers of identical sizes and small lockers above with a picture of a shoe on each door. We twigged. We placed our smart, leather shoes in the locker and slid our toes into the cheaper offerings. Too big for me. Too small for him. I no longer looked elegant in my pencil-slim skirt. A lean, dark-haired, almond-eyed beauty, dressed in a kimono, materialised and bowed. A worried frown spread across her forehead. A torrent of sweet nothings issued from her carefully painted lips. Dumb expressions, then smiles from us. Our reservation card (acquired on our behalf by a young student) was shown and a book produced in return. Just sign here was obvious – but which way and how? Previous guests had drawn lovely characters down the pages. What should we do? Our visiting card was whisked out and we laboriously copied our names in Katakana (the phonic Japanese script invented for Western words) down the page with a brush and ink. How huge and untidy ours looked compared to the other artistic attempts! The Oriental beauty read our symbols out loud. They were our names. Incredible!

We were escorted along familiar red-carpeted corridors to a door, the key was turned and we were ushered in. She slid out of her brown, plastic mules, we did the same. In bare feet we walked onto the tatami-matted floor. The rice-plant stems of the mat felt springy and warm. She slid open paper-covered, wooden screens, bowed and left us alone.

We stared. An almost empty room. A low table was in the middle with a pink-flowered duvet spread over it and two legless chairs on each side. On top of the duvet a vacuum flask and a round wooden box. On removing the beautiful lacquered lid we discovered two cups and a pot of tea-leaves. Ah! Refreshment! No milk, no sugar but two welcome cups of green tea. We sat on the strange chairs and our feet and legs slid under the duvet. It was warm and cosy. An electric heater was underneath. What luxury!

Our eyes looked around the edges of the room, where the tatami failed to reach. An alcove held a vase of flowers and a large scroll de-picting more strange characters hung above it. A television, a tele-phone, two toothbrushes and paste, and two minute towels were all we could see. No beds. No washbasins. No bath. No toilet. HELP!

It came by telephone. No-one wanted to answer it. What would the voice say? Would we understand? Courage failed us. We ignored it. So a few minutes later a knock came on the door instead. A different kimono and a different face entered. A screen was slid open and a pile of bedding was dragged out. Two thin mattresses, two pillows, two duvets were spread on the hay-like floor in seconds. On top were care-fully placed two navy and white cotton dressing gowns, pristinely starched and ironed. A finger beckoned – we followed – pausing long enough to slip back into those plastic shoes. We were ushered into the toilet at the end of the corridor. Shoes off – wooden clogs on. We were both led past the urinals to a door and through it to a hole in a tiled floor. Please face the cistern when using it, was demonstrated to us!

Shoes exchanged again and down to the basement. The double doors kept in the steam but not the smell. Bad eggs? A gas leak? No, it was sulphur. The steam engulfed us as it rose from the natural hot spring bubbling in through the wall and into a large, rock-edged, round pool. The bath. A superb mime was enacted by our hostess. Your clothes go in the cubby hole, you sit on the pink plastic stool, you pick up the scoop and slosh water from a tap all over you and use the pink soap. Rinse yourself off and obviously the floor too! Then you step between the rocks and relax in the steaming cauldron. Her role as an actress finished, she bowed and retreated to the clear air out-side. We were alone – perhaps we should have gone to the Hilton. No. Let's use it now. No-one around. We can experiment alone. We did. It was marvellous.

Upstairs, clean and relaxed, we put on our flowery cotton *yukatas*. Great hilarity. Six foot of Western male, with hairy legs protruding from a knee-length gown, is a funny sight.

It must be supper time. We're hungry. What fun, embarrassment or confusion was in store now? A knock on the door, a beckoning finger again. We followed to the dining room. Thirty identically clad Japanese were sitting on their feet on cushions at low, low tables. They stopped eating. They stared. They bowed. They smiled. We smiled and bowed and sat like them whilst trying to keep our modesty with the buttonless gowns. Twenty-two small dishes faced us, offering about forty-four pretty but unidentifiable morsels. Who does the washing-up was my first thought! What to try first? We surreptitiously looked around to our fellow diners. It didn't seem to matter. We settled for the items that were easier to catch with our wooden chopsticks. We were very puzzled by some of the strange tastes. An elderly lady near us spoke. "You are English? Welcome. I will tell you what you eat. Raw horse meat, chopped horseradish, raw tuna, seaweed, fish paste cake, chrysanthemum leaves, tofu, squid . . ."

She pointed out and named each bite-sized titbit. We wished she hadn't told us. Ignorance was bliss! Sake flowed, beer abounded and we relaxed yet again. So unfortunately did our poor feet. The pins and needles were excruciating. Inexpert and slow, we finished last. We tried to stand on our numb feet and painfully hobbled out to the immaculate, miniature Japanese garden, where we strolled in silence with the strangely uniformed clan of fellow travellers in the spring warmth.

Now for bed. We passed open doors along that carpeted corridor and irresistibly peeped in. Some were lying in their beds still wearing their bathrobes and watching television. That's what we'd do. Clad in our flowery gowns we snuggled down, laid our heads on the hard, rice-husk pillows and watched Prince Charles and Princess Diana touring Japan. Were they experiencing the *real* Japan, like us?

MARTIN BROWN

TRINIDAD THEN TOBAGO

The T-shirt bemoaning "another day in bloody Paradise" is an amusing souvenir for tourists to Barbados. For cooped-up expatriates, however, the message has a hollower ring, and periodic sorties from the island are essential to the sanity. Choosing a destination is one thing, but arranging a holiday is another. Travel agents here are precisely what the name implies, purveyors of airline tickets. They have no holiday brochures to browse through on sultry winter evenings; their hotel guides are three years out of date; and their packaged tours are confined to burgers in Disneyworld, shopping trips to Caracas and dirty weekends in Rio. To them, Machu Picchu is probably a new rum cocktail.

The Trinidad and Tobago Tourist Board in Port-of-Spain is no better: it didn't even reply to our request for tourist literature. But we are by now well used to Caribbean incompetence. We were to spend the first few days with friends in Trinidad, so we booked a Tobago guesthouse by phone, rubbed our hands at the timely devaluation of the TT dollar and packed cozzies, kaolin and cockroach killer.

Arriving in Trinidad on the inevitably delayed flight, we headed south from the airport across the Caroni plain, a patchwork of vigorous weeds and stunted sugar cane, dotted with sleazy snackettes and squalid stilt houses, worlds away from the bright rumshops and neatly painted chattel houses of Barbados. The only colour came from garish Hindu temples and the clusters of tatty prayer flags fluttering from bamboo poles, reminding us that half Trinidad's population can trace its origins to the indentured labourers lured over from India after the abolition of slavery.

Our friends, Baptist missionaries running theological training courses for local pastors, live near San Fernando. A miserable town backing on to a mud shore and an oily sea, its peeling municipal edifices, derelict building sites and burglar-barred shopfronts testify to the economic and aesthetic depression of the south. Whites like us, far from the expat enclaves of Port-of-Spain, provided a diversion for unemployed and homeless loiterers as we took in the landmarks (defoliated hill, gaunt Victorian hospital, sprawling graveyard). The "Last train to San Fernando", commemorated in a 1950s pop song, stands in the main square: those who missed it were indeed fortunate.

It drizzled steadily on our excursions. At a Baptist church service our eight-year-old son beat a hasty retreat, deafened by carols lustily sung to a beat marked by handclaps and tambourines, and frightened by an old lady who lurched around in a trance proclaiming the glories of the Lord to approving Alleluias from the congregation. We visited the unique pitch lake discovered by Sir Walter Raleigh, who failed to notice its resemblance to a razed slag heap. We peered at birds through the gloom of a sodden nature reserve. We discovered too late that to rent a car in Trinidad you need an International Driving Permit. And we spent a whole morning locked in battle with the chronic telephone system to reconfirm our flights out. (The phone won.)

Old Year's Night was truly memorable. Planning to retire early, we celebrated the British New Year at 8pm with a cup of coffee (there are *some* drawbacks to having Baptist friends). The party-goers next door had other plans for us, though, and drowned the World Service with their megawatts. The midnight air was split by the wailing of the oil refinery's siren, and the house foundations finally came to rest at 3.45am. New Year's resolution: we will *not* go to Trinidad for Carnival.

Tobago, when we finally arrived after the customary flight cancellations and engine troubles, was a delight compared with its ghastly sister. Small, rural, uncrowded and friendly, it has a grace and charm untypical of the Caribbean. Coconut palms grow everywhere, a welcome change from the sugar cane landscape of Barbados. The beaches are magnificent, particularly on the sheltered north-west coast. Pigeon Point Bay could pass as the film set for Robinson Crusoe. Palms lean over turquoise water and silver sands, and we had the place to ourselves most of the morning, until a large cruise liner hove to beyond the reef and disgorged an armada of lifeboats full of fat, unquiet Americans, who stood in line for their beach towels, fumigated the beach bar with cigars and hogged the pedalos. We beat a hasty retreat.

The weather was kinder here: Tobago was breezy and bright. From the sloping gardens of Fort King George, bastion of successive French and English garrisons in the eighteenth century, the view of the rugged east coast was rewarding. In our rented car (Tobago doesn't worry about international permits) we braved roads composed entirely of landslides and craters to reach the hilltown of Moriah, centre of a tropical Tuscany, surrounded by sloping groves of bananas, palms and red Immortelle trees. We rubbernecked the roof of photographer Norman Parkinson's home and chatted to his gardener, watering cows from a coolbox. A glass-bottomed boat took us to the famous Buccoo reef at low tide, where snorkelling among the angelfish, parrotfish and living corals is absorbing. At the elegant Arnos Vale hotel our children made a valiant attempt to scare away the brightly-coloured birds which come to share afternoon tea with a discreetly rich and well-dressed American and German clientèle.

The guesthouse brought us back to earth. In this creole Fawlty Towers the translucent towels were all we needed after bathing in a shower that merely dribbled water ("the maids haven't complained about it"); bare-bulb ceiling lights didn't work even when I accepted the kind offer of a stepladder to fix them myself; the swimming pool was empty and would remain so for six weeks until the island's only pool technician returned from his holiday in the UK to mend it; and an afternoon ice-cream for the children was provided only on condition that my wife and I agreed to forgo our share at dinner. The proprietress wasn't expecting us until the day after we arrived, but her impromptu home-made spread of pumpkin soup, spicy meatballs, creole fish and guava ice-cream was delicious. The planned menu for subsequent nights, however, reflected a more international cuisine of packeted soup, chicken-free pilau and tinned fruit salad.

Guesthouse apart, Tobago's main dampeners of the holiday spirit are having to transit at Piarco airport in Trinidad, and BWIA's stranglehold on air transport. The acronym of Trinidad's loss-making national carrier is reputed to mean "but will it arrive?" and we duly took five-and-a-half hours to travel the 200-odd miles back to Barbados. The trip would at least have been more eventful two days later: Tobago's little airfield was closed for a bomb scare, while concurrently at Piarco a mental hospital outpatient bypassed security and rode a motorbike up the runway towards an oncoming jet.

JULIA BUTT

LES MALHEUREUSES

Napeoleon greeted us when we arrived in the palm-fringed port of Ajaccio and disembarked onto the jetty. Corsica's capital exhibits boulevards, bars and boats in honour of its most famous son. The white-glossed vessels glide out slowly with their cargoes of rich French and Italian mariners, perhaps south to Sardinia or Sicily before venturing upon Poseidon's homeland in the depths of the Aegean.

We wound up into the mountains for three hours at the back of a stifling minibus, rucksacks on knees, to arrive at Petreto-Bicchisano to au-pair and keep shop for two months. The villages of bleached stone are perched on crags, almost indistinguishable in the dense green forests. Grey stones on distant, wispy mountaintops become crosses and tombstones as one ascends. Every village has its protective saint and little dark chapel. Children play in the street with its one-thousand-foot drop to the bronze river below. The old women in black do not shout warnings. It seems that one is born to Corsica with an instinct of its precariousness.

The Bungelmi family are politicians, part of the recently-formed Corsican Assembly, which gave devolution to this tiny French *départe-ment*. They are like God to the villagers; we, as their servants and the only *"anglaises"* (actually *"écossaises"* and therefore even more rarified) to have visited this mountain ledge are held in high esteem. Once it is established that our guttural French accents are not of German origin they are our friends. Old wars die hard.

The Wild Man of the Woods stops us as we climb the steep mountains, pushing Denis in his baby buggy (imported from le Continent or mainland France) to see his cousins in the next village five hundred feet due north.

"You are the English girls," he says. "What is it like now?"

When asked if he has visited our country, he smiles sadly and says in English with a touch of Geordie, "I was in the British Navy in the Second World War. It was too much. I deserted ship at Marseilles and came here to hide. This is the first time I've spoken English in forty years."

He continues down the mountain to his wooden shack and his bees.

Our Corsican charges are bandits born to shriek and howl all day in the white heat. Their parents are on the point of divorce. The primordial sense of God so strong in these ancient villages has no pull on the young Corsicans who escape to the sophistication of Paris to marry in register offices. After all, why worry about Heaven when Paradise has been experienced first hand on this Ile de Beauté? We are caught in the middle of theatrical scenes beginning with Roland's selfishness in bed and ending with Marie-Laure throwing a runny round of ewe's cheese against the wall. Drama being the simplest form of communication, we quickly pick up the Corsican dialect! The atmosphere explodes every hot evening and echoes round the valley so we run away in the middle of the night. There are no street lights so we walk in the middle of the road to avoid hidden scorpions on the grassy banks. In the distance the the mountains glow like coal embers to light our way. The forest fires have begun – shall we escape before they reach our ridge?

Having hitched to the capital we make camp on the beach in the early morning. We have another job by lunchtime – waitresses in a nightclub. This solves the accommodation problem. We can work by night and sleep by day on the beach, leaving Mathieu, the old man who sleeps in his beach café, to guard our rucksacks. Our pretty floral sundresses and espadrilles look out of place in the red-lit club beside the glittering harbour where the waitresses wear black rubber and gold chains. There is only male clientèle. As foreign blonds we are greatly in demand – we stay behind the bar nervously washing the same glasses whilst the black rubber girls mingle, dance and suction on to the customers, giggling at our behaviour. Madame Catya pokes us crossly and tells us to circulate but the conversation is disjointed:

"The mountains, the sun and the beaches are so beautiful here," I attempt to a hotel tycoon.

"Your tits are like great big melons," he replies, smiling.

I wonder if I have misunderstood, but when his counterpart signs a cheque for £150 for a glass of Perrier and Caroline, I know it's time to make another escape, the second in twenty-four hours.

My twentieth birthday present from Caroline is a secondhand 1963 military blanket on which to sleep on the beach. On our first night under the stars we awake to blinding torches and Inspector Clouseau, who moves us on. We sit in the eerie square at 3am with Napoleon looking down menacingly for half an hour and then return to the beach to sleep until morning.

Fabienne wakes us. She is pretty in a New York Jewish sort of way – cracked nose, olive skin, beautiful drooping eyes with lots of kohl, smoker's teeth and bitten nails. Wrapped in a peasant blanket she talks of *"le business"* in Soho and Piccadilly – prostitution to pay for her drug addiction. Her arms are scars, dead veins with hanging skin which will take no more abuse, and so her ankles have become the focal point of her masochism. Corsica is vacation after hospitalisation in Amsterdam and, more importantly from her point of view, stamping ground of many Moroccans who come from the hash crops of North Africa to supply France from this paradise isle.

Mathieu now lets us sleep under the tables in his café and feeds us coffee and croissants. In return we fetch his one hundred baguettes steaming from the bakery in the silver dawn in one huge basket which feeds the beach at lunchtime. Then we jog behind the French Legion whose Mediterranean base is in the hills at Cap Corse. The annoyed P.T. instructor quickens the pace and we soon fall behind in the 8am heat. Bottled water for lunch. Jasmine tea from flasks with the learned Chinese Parisians from the Sorbonne as an afternoon ritual. Then more bottled water (by this time boiling) until the beach is empty and we light our gas burner to boil eggs for supper.

"Look at what happens to the bad boys and girls," a man warns his little son as they stare at us over the beach wall.

The ferry arrives with new beach bums and we play guitar and sing *American Pie* into the night, although none of us wants to look any further for the Promised Land. Richard arrives from trekking in the Sahara with another burner so we feast on pasta and ratatouille.

The next day we decide that haircuts are in order. Someone produces nail scissors and a Swiss Army knife and the Ajaccio set look on in horror as we create Sassoon's on Sea. A German under the next parasol who works for *Der Spiegel* takes photographs while the New Assymmetric is being created. We hear Mathieu tell the old town codgers that he feels duty bound to help us, *"les jeunes malheureuses"*.

We live on fifteen francs a day but still lend our precious coins to an English family for their taxi fare back to the next resort when we meet them arguing noisily in the main square under the fountains. They return to our home on the beach the next day with the money and two bottles of wine. Everything is shared in this communal society we have founded – food, advice, confidences, waterlogged newspapers and our bible, *Hitch-hiker's Guide to Europe*. We shower under the cold hosepipe on the beach yet become accustomed to our permanent sandy skins. We swim all day to keep cool and only when our faces blister do we long for a tiled villa with dark recesses instead of our parasols. We have lost our Aberdeen granite looks and are now sinewy, lean, mahogany animals used to twenty-four hours a day in the open air and terrified of enclosure.

We travel to Bonifacio, the southernmost tip of Corsica. Huge sedimentary rocks rise as high as cliffs out of the sea, having fallen from the mainland centuries ago. The town juts out of the cliffs and seems in danger of tumbling into the blue-green *algue* below. We watch the flat, barren coast of Sardinia twelve kilometres across the strait enviously. Another land to discover but the fifteen franc ferry crossing is a whole day's survival.

And so the summer draws to a close as the money runs out. We pack up our temporary home and leave the Island to face another year of law school. *Malheureuses?* Perhaps now, yes.

ANNE BONVILLE WERE

THE START OF A JOURNEY

How many people had made this journey before me? Thousands upon thousands. The thought that I was travelling in distinquished company never crossed my mind as I looked at the pale, drawn faces in the early dawn of the Gatwick departure lounge. I remembered my daughter's long, pale, damp toes covered in grass clippings when we had been swimming before school, part of the "get trim for the holiday" programme. I remembered the evenings spent reading while muscles jerked convulsively to the rhythm of the Slendertone, passive exerciser, part of the same programme. I remembered, with distaste, the little green goggles you must wear when using a sun-lamp.

In the aircraft, to accompany the plastic food, the wedding of Prince Andrew flickered on the screen; the sub-titles were in Italian. At Rhodes Airport two long queues straggled in silence in the blazing sun, inching forward to Immigration. Inside, the heat was oppressive as bodies packed tightly together waited for luggage which was long in coming. In the Ladies, a notice said all toilet paper must be deposited in the bucket provided and not flushed away. The bucket was empty.

Couriers in uniform have badges with their Christian names on. Your name is on their list. Hot buses. "Leave your luggage here. Come back at seven." We sit outside a café, under palm trees. We walk by the harbour and talk of people we knew years ago. I feel at home here. Old men sitting together on benches greet us courteously. I *am* at home here. At seven we sail out of the harbour past the remains of the Colossus. This is the start of a journey which I now know will take me the rest of my life.

It is dark when the boat nears Symi. The island is completely dark. The air grows very hot. Suddenly, there are the lights of Pedi winking at the end of the bay. Then, as we round the last headland, we see the lights of Symi town sharply climbing the hillside. It is beautiful. There could be no better way to arrive anywhere than to sail towards lights like these.

In the harbour the boat swings slowly round to dock stern first. Tavernas line the quayside. Behind them, dotting the hillside, are the neo-classical houses built by the sponge traders. No high-rise blocks, no jarring modern note. This cannot be real. We have strayed onto some beautiful stage set. Yet on the quay all is bustle as a week's supplies are off-loaded. We find Alison and set off with her in this joyful throng for the Villa Panormitis. It is tucked away on a little square behind the Ionian and Popular Bank of Greece.

The flat is spotless but spartan. We freshen up then go back to the harbour, a two-minute walk. Courteously the waiters invite us to dine in their restaurants. They invite us to inspect the kitchens. The tables are a few feet from the water. Every restaurant serves fish: sole, bream, swordfish, calamares, sardines, grilled prawns, snapper. We start our meal with tomato salad.

Always beside you when you eat are the cats. They creep up silently, surreptitiously, and sit staring with huge shining eyes. They are not like English cats. They are thin and elegant and their ancestors posed for Egyptian sculptors. They wait patiently for the fish heads, skins and even skeletons which the tourists always throw them.

The day starts early on Symi, around five. A single cock is answered until the din is deafening. Donkeys and goats join in. Soon there are people in the street who talk loudly. *"Kálimerá sas."* The bare hills grow pink, the houses painted in shades of honey, apricot, peach, ochre and burnt sienna glow. This is the best time. The sound of hooves as the donkey train trots past. There are few cars, just one or two trucks and taxis which travel over the hill on the new road to Pedi. But the bells in the basilica ring early. So much noise, so much vitality.

Our balcony overlooked the square. Every morning we sat there and had our breakfast, yogurt mixed with honey and warm poppy-seed rolls fresh from the baker. Every evening, as the sun was setting, we sat there with a gin and tonic before going out. On our balcony we became part of the life of Greece.

Directly underneath was the chemist. The tourists came for suntan creams and films for cameras, but the people of Symi often seemed to gather for a chat or for the diagnosis of some minor complaint. Sometimes the sick would sit on the steps which led up to the centre of the square. Were they enthralled by the beauty of the lady pharmacist, or merely waiting for her medicine to take effect?

The house opposite was like some child's cardboard toy, for in the early morning you could see into all the rooms before they closed the shutters to keep out the heat. In a strange way I shared their life, watched them watering their plants, smelt their coffee and the incense which they burnt on Sundays. They used the square as an extension to their house and sat on the steps or brought out chairs. They talked loudly, joyously, continually. The young daughters in white dresses poured water over their feet. The grandmothers played with the babies.

Janni Kalafatis ran the souvenir shop near the chemist, described on his carrier bags as a "sort of novelty shop". He told me that the temperature was reaching 40°C in the afternoons inside his house. "Much too hot," he said.

But in the afternoons we basked on rocks or sought shade under gnarled olive trees. And swam and swam and swam.

We explored the island from north to south and east to west. We went along thyme-scented goat tracks to Agios Nicolaios. We took a taxi to Pedi squashed together with a priest who smelt of herbs. We travelled by truck to Panormitis, hanging on for dear life as it lurched its way over the boulder-strewn track, in places inches from the edge.

We visited the Monastery of Saint Michael, the great healer. Hibiscus and tamarisk grow in the courtyard paved with a mosaic of pebbles. In the dim basilica hundreds of brass lamps are suspended from the ceiling. The tourists burn candles, icons reflecting their light. Little metal tags hang on one wall, each with a picture of a part of the body, left there by pilgrims seeking a cure.

Often we sailed on the *Triton* with Captain Sotaris to Marathounda, Sesklia or Agios Emilianos. Remote, inaccessible bays like the pictures in the travel agents' brochures. All the boatmen serve slices of watermelon and the passengers spit the pips into the sea.

Colin sat near the water wearing only his dead wife's sunhat. I sat in the shade of a tiny church and read Plato's account of the death of Socrates, Penguin edition. The first steps of another journey. At lunchtime Captain Sotaris, helped by his sons, prepared a barbecue. Grilled chicken and lamb, salads in washing-up bowls, and feta cheese. When it was ready he called "Wine time", and served white wine in paper cups from a jerrican.

In the evening we sit on the balcony under the stars. The stars are brighter here and have seen other sorrows. This thought helps put things in perspective, to give our lives a sense of proportion.

Then we are back at the airport. Mess everywhere. At the same table three English youths with "No Problem" emblazoned on their T-shirts read the *Sun*. In the Ladies, this time, the bucket overflows with used loo paper.

I think of our square and the basilica at the far end. I think of the Friday morning I joined the small congregation.

The priest wears a pale blue cope, blue the colour of Greece. There are six women and myself. I stand at the door. Incense fills the air, the women sing the responses. The priest blesses the bread and the women go into the sanctuary to receive it. One of them comes and shares hers with me.

At Gatwick it is raining.

TRACING THE SPANISH CONNECTION

01:45 on October 28th, Alicante airport was at 14°C. Early-morning arrivals are better than late evening as a civilised bed does not seem necessary. Instead, easy resignation to the large, cushioned lounge seats.

Head down, "lights-out". Time to reflect the snap decision to take a premature "bucket" seat the day before departure. Leaving Britain's dismal weather had some influence. The airport announcement system reaches every corner with admirable efficiency. Not much sleep.

Bus to Alicante, dump the gear and straight for the beach with three women met at the *pension* – two Canadians, one American. Warm sand, sunning bodies and a beckoning sea. In the late afternoon we strolled up to the castle for a panorama of informative views. The sunset was orange and warm.

Torrevieja, some one hour south by bus, was on the following day's agenda. The American, Cindy, joined in, so we sat together in a busy bus which carried us out through Alicante's industrial area to dry, dusty countryside bearing some cotton plantations and commercial salt pans.

Our destination is in south-east Spain, between the capes of Pila and Prima, surrounded by two large, natural, saltwater lagoons. Torrevieja has some 14,000 inhabitants and produces more than 800,000 tons of salt a year. That is the principal industry; tourism comes next. In bygone days it was a great shipbuilding port and this was the reason for my visit – to trace the history of one of its offspring, the *Pascual Flores*, a 126-foot, three-masted trading schooner built there in 1919, now undergoing renovation in England.

On arrival, Cindy headed for the beach, I to improve my knowledge of the town. That evening, a moonlit picnic of cheese, wine, shrimps and bread on a whitewashed, concrete bench, set among the rocks fifteen feet from the Mediterranean, served to bid bon voyage to the travelling American. Next day she left, heading for Granada, and I began my investigations.

The local yacht club seemed a good place to start. Quite a place, too.

A stumpy, mahogany-and-brass ship's relic, a compass-bearer produced by Kelvin, Bottomley & Baird Ltd of Cambridge Street, Glasgow, greets you as you enter the foyer.

The radio-officer-cum-receptionist prepared a list of "old seadogs" and other useful bodies for me. A book entitled *Los Ultimos Veleros del Mediterráneo,* cataloguing much of the area's seagoing history, was offered on loan, so I retreated to the boiling patio, armed with a cold beer and pocket Spanish dictionary. More time was spent soaking up the sun and watching the local rowing club training than studying the text, but I could return to that.

The following morning I made a start on the list. The first two people were not at home but the third, Torrevieja's official historian, answered the doorbell of his comfortable apartment. A Spaniard in his mid-thirties, apparently a doctor, with signs of children scattered among the leatherbound furniture. Together we viewed his collection of old ships' photographs and he provided the address of another old seaman, José Hurtado, for my list.

My luck was in with señor Hurtado, who answered his buzzer with a gruff greeting – as you would expect of a tough old seaman when confronted by some strange tourist. But "Pepe Felicia" changed his expression from cold to warm when he heard the words "Pascual Flores". A large left hand, placed reassuringly below my right shoulder blade, ushered me into his simple apartment.

Ships' models, nautical photos, charts and drawings adorned the surfaces. This seventy-five-year-old, short, stocky ex-seaman makes highly intricate models in his retirement. More specifically he was a marine engineer, and my own marine engineering experiences allowed us immediate, enthusiastic exchanges.

The accuracy, authenticity and detail of his work was a treat for the eye and mind. Most of his models are in wood – teak, for example, which he prepares on machine tools built from the gizzards of old washing machines. He models steel ships in copper, starting with wooden forms, and has produced glass-fibre models of contemporary racing sloops. Eighteen months were spent on a galleon, the plans and dimensions coming from a seventeenth-century text kept in a London museum, which he arranged to photo-copy. On average he will spend eight months on a wooden sailing ship.

After two hours we parted with an arrangement to meet next day at the office of a local, semi-retired sailmaker, Juan Bautista Buades, *El Maestro Velero de Torrevieja,* where José would arrange for a group of old seamen to be in attendance. My "visits" list suddenly shrank to nothing.

Across the boulevard from the Yacht Club I stumbled upon the Bar Tiburón, where a small collection of old sailing photographs occupies some wall-space. Ignoring the locals' questioning glances, I strained to read, then note, some inscriptions, before settling down to a cold drink.

There had been two main shipbuilding sites in Torrevieja. The shipyard of Antonio Mari, where *Pascual Flores* was built, has been tarmacked for car-parking and port offices; the other, a stretch of beach to the south of town, is still occasionally used. As luck would have it, a 26-metre, two-mast schooner was in the early stages of construction. Apparently it was for a Tenerife-based, English charter company. Traditional methods, including adzes, are still used to whittle the Spanish pine to lines similar to those of her forebears.

The rendezvous at the sailmaker's found seven old gents sitting in a circle on various odd seats. Others came and went during the morning, but there was one notable absentee, Francisco Mari, "El Temporal", whom I understand to have been a captain of *Pascual Flores*.

The relationship of sail-types to hull-form was given much attention after I disclosed that plans were afoot to modify *Pascual Flores'* rig to include two square fore-topsails. Originally she was built as a *paillebot* (schooner), rigged with *velas de cuchillas* (literally translating as knife sails) as opposed to *velas de cuadros* (square sails). *Cuchillas* are for speed, *cuadros* for power. Apparently, the bow form associated with square sails is fat compared to the slim bow of schooners. Hence the addition of these sails to a schooner requires considerable re-analysis of the rigging, and possibly necessitates the reduction and relocation of the masts. In certain rough conditions square sails, particularly foretops, could drive a ship under. At this point I recalled the loss of the *Marquesa*, off Bermuda, during the 1984 Tall Ships Race. They had known her well, indicating that she too had been a *paillebot*, ie schooner-rigged. Did the *Marquesa* not have some square sails when lost?

One eighty-one-year-old seaman, who had crewed the *Carmen Flores*, sister ship of *Pascual Flores*, related that the latter's maiden voyage was to Cuba with a cargo of salt, returning with a load of mahogany, and that she was capable of speeds up to eight knots.

A further meeting was arranged for the following afternoon, which should include a visit to a private collection of maritime memorabilia situated in the attic of a modern apartment nearby.

Next morning I tried Francisco Mari's house once more, having failed to raise him on the first day. The local butcher said he should be in so, after ringing, I banged my fist on the door. Success. I was getting used to the initial reaction, but the magic words "Pascual Flores" worked a treat.

We set to at the dinner table, gradually feeding questions until the old man found his own rhythm. "El Temporal" was born in 1906 and went to sea aboard *Pascual Flores* in 1919. By the age of sixteen he was

The good ship *Pascual Flores* under sail. *(Tracing the Spanish Connection)*

A two-mast schooner under construction in Torrevieja. *(Tracing the Spanish Connection)*

ship's mate, apparently due in part to the untimely departure of his predecessor; and at thirty-four he was promoted to captain.

Apparently, someone had visited him four years previously, enquiring of the ship. Whoever it was had agreed to send up-to-date material on his old command, but to date he had received nothing. Was this the reason for his absence yesterday? Until now I was led to believe that no photographs existed of the ship under sail, but to my delight there was one on his wall. Arranging to copy his old photos and setting up a portrait of himself proved easier than expected.

The old man related that a film, *La última cita* (The last appointment), was made around 1936 using the *Pascual Flores*. An actress, Carmen Flores, starred and the producer was one Ricardo Gargullo of the Casa Gaumont Production House in Barcelona.

The ship's conversion into a rather ugly motor sailer in 1956 caused "El Temporal" to part company with her. His next and last ship, the *Ramone Freisas,* was a three-mast *paillebot* like his first.

Because I was getting interested, I tried him on the subject of the *Marquesa* – he knew both it and its sister ship, *Ciudad de Inca,* which is still sailing. Señor Mari recalled that neither of them originally had any square sails. We parted with my promising to send information of his old ship.

The meeting at the sailmaker's involved examining albums of photographs and referring to the book *Los Ultimos Veleros del Mediterráneo,* which was written by a close friend of theirs, José Huertas Morion, a resident of Valencia. The private museum was not accessible that day, and in fact it continued to elude me, despite arranging another date.

Dinner that evening with some Brits, was a local speciality which we had prearranged with a small bar. *Lubina,* a fish of some three pounds with nasty-looking teeth, was covered with a half-inch layer of salt, then oven-baked till the salt was rock hard. Organise some salads, crack the "cover" off the fish, the top off a bottle of white Rioja, and the world soared up an octave.

I was privileged to join the circle at the sailmaker's several more times over the next few days and, when I finally bade them farewell, received a small rope ornament as a memento of our times together. Perhaps the team renovating the *Pascual Flores,* in Bristol, should invite them over to pass on some of their knowledge and experience which they are so willing to share. I'm sure the old men would appreciate an outlet for their living archive of seamanship and traditional shipbuilding.

Torrevieja itself came across as a town divided. On one side the old generation of ex-seamen, shipbuilders and fishermen; and on the other

Upwards and onwards. (*Midnight on Mt Blanc*)

the new tourist-orientated business-people of the hotels, bars and shops. The latter extracted your money rather smartly, and the goods in return were not always as expected.

My return to Alicante served to reinforce these observations. There the atmosphere is more open – due in part, I'm sure, to its being more cosmopolitan. The people are friendly and helpful.

Visit Alicante's castles for the views, seek out the old town, eat in backstreet restaurants where the *menú del día* will test your storage capacity, tickle your palate and not collapse your purse. The main food market has to be sampled just to see and feel the buzz, if not to buy. It is so alive, such a density of colour and activity, that you can spend a morning just walking around.

The city's nightlife happens in the old quarter where an amazing proliferation of little bars, with simple decor and quality sound systems, compete for the attention of the trendy, image-conscious locals who come out to play after ten o'clock in the evening. The cobbled streets and squares, lit by quaint wall-lamps, served to entertain as we navigated our mesmerised way through into the early hours.

Next stop, Barcelona. But that's another story.

R. G. WILLIS

MIDNIGHT ON MONT BLANC

Depression lurked over me like a Lakeland storm-sky: oppressive, inevitable and apparently unending. "What you need," said Bernie over the top of his beer, "is to take your mind off it; get out onto the hill. Let's go and climb Mont Blanc. We can drive down on your bike."

The suggestion seemed suitably absurd – neither of us had done any serious climbing for a decade and I had never done any work on snow and ice. So we went. Friends took the heavy gear in a car. (I had failed to accommodate two full sets of climbing equipment, a tent, books and spare clothes in the panniers of my new BMW and felt slightly cheated.) On the open roads, the apparently deserted French *péages,* I relished the lack of baggage and flew south.

We stopped at service stations for coffee and short rests in the sun, parking among the admiring summer super-bikers. I quickly fell into old habits as the cameraderie of the motorcycle fraternity reasserted itself – a quick flash of the headlamp as you pass at high speed, a full wave to the rider of another BMW, the critically admiring glances over the ranks of other machines, the knowledgeable chatter of performance figures, and the bullshit of personal near misses and friends lost.

Chamonix, when we arrived, was hot, expensive and distractingly full of beautiful women. We drank beer and listened to tales of the good old days when our boys fought the French climbers in the streets, and won. Beside the bar, Maurice counted the takings, his blind eyes having seen it all. We took to the hills.

"I know an easy route to do as an introduction," said Mick, "the Traverse de Dômes des Miage." We conferred and studied maps. To my untutored eye the route looked long but straightforward, and I nonchalantly agreed. After a sleepless night in the dormitory of an alpine hut we set out at 3am. The fresh pre-dawn air was a luxury in comparison with the foetid heat of the bunks, and the stars were brilliant in the black, black sky. As we walked up to the glacier I felt, for the first time in months, glad to be alive.

I felt worse, later. The route took fourteen hours and wrecked my feet. For most of the way it was a long plod up the glacier, an interminable slope of ice and snow. My borrowed crampons fell to pieces and my new boots were too large. The clear night sky gave way to a perfect day and Bernie, who had forgotten a hat, nearly died of sunstroke. At the highest point we rested and ate a snack. I looked around at the peaks and across at the bulk of Mont Blanc, looming above us. "It'll be easy," said Mick, following my gaze. "We'll do the standard route; get the train out of the valley and walk up to the Gautier hut for a sleep, then get up at midnight and be on the summit for dawn. Mind you," he added as he effortlessly set off down the slope, "it may be crowded. This year is the two-hundredth anniversary of its first ascent."

I finished my chocolate and followed him, my crampons, blisters and fear making me hesitant. Below me the snow slope steepened, a long seductive white arc ending abruptly in . . . My mind wandered. I imagined a slip and the gathering speed, the futile inexperienced attempts to stop myself with the axe, a moment's despair and then capitulation to fate as I hurtled over the edge into an unbroken, terminally exhilarating, one-way flight to the glacier 4,000 feet below.

Bernie pulled on the rope and cursed me for stopping; I plodded on. My feet hurt.

Four days later, the train heaved its way out of the valley towards the end of the Bionnassay Glacier. Through the glass I stared at the pine trees and the brilliant meadow flowers. The carriage filled with the perfume of tourists, up for the day, and the sweat of climbers, rucksacks balanced on their knees, all heading for the Blanc. When the track wound alongside a cliff the small girl sitting opposite looked out in disbelief as the trees gave way to nothing. She pulled her eyes away in fear and looked around the train – the view there was worse, rucksacks, hairy knees, ice-axes, unshaven climbers lost in contemplation of the weather.

We arrived at the top station and the train disgorged. Tourists wandered slowly across to the café or to the viewing platform from which they could look up at the great bleak sweep of the mountain opposite. Down the valley the world became more sane, as the stone desert below the glacier gave way to meadows and woodland.

The climbers had no time for niceties. A hundred packs were shouldered and a long queue of people marched purposefully up the track which, like a motorway, led uphill from the station. I looked in horror – was this the beautiful isolation of the mountains about which I had been told for years? Heavy boots crushed the life out of any remaining plants and sent small showers of stones down onto the people below. Walkers jockeyed for position on the network of tracks which zigzagged up the first slope. The hillside crumbled visibly under the onslaught, and I couldn't help but think of the devastation which has been wrought on British mountains by a similar recreational assaults.

Beside the path was a small hut, a shelter for hunters, and standing around it was a group of chamoix waiting, like the sheep on Helvellyn, for the tourists who would photograph and feed them. The climbers pressed on oblivious. Bernie stopped me and pointed forwards. Ahead, a long long way ahead, and at the top of a seemingly vertical rock face, was a silver blob. "The Gautier," he panted, "about four and a half thousand feet above us. Three and a half thousand vertically from there to the summit." I nodded and we walked on in the heat as the sun grew higher in the sky. "Mad dogs and Englishmen," I thought, but I couldn't see the dogs.

The hut appeared to get no closer. We walked and scrambled, gradually passing most of the others who had come up with us on the train. Our chances of getting a sleeping space seemed remote even without the crowds who were following us, and I had no wish to sleep outside on the ground. In the early afternoon we came to the foot of the final climb to the hut. Below us to the right, across the glacier, was another hut, the Tête Sauvage. Someone there was playing a flute and the sound blended beautifully with the superb landscape. Some of the walkers began to go that way, not lured by the Pied Piper, but to spend the night at a lower altitude and to use the Tête Sauvage as the springboard for their attempt on the summit the following morning.

As we climbed upward, the cloud began to close in and I wondered if the following day would be too bad for the attempt – the summit can be swept by winds of 100mph. Bernie had tried this route twice before and each time the weather had forced him back. We passed a rusty iron cross, a memorial to a dead climber, and finally reached the hut, a metal-skinned structure perched on the cliff edge. Already people were staking claims to places on the ground, and when I opened the door I knew why. A waft of hot sweaty air hit me and a pile of rucksacks threatened to follow. I edged my way inside.

Tony and Mick were perched on a bench at the back of the room surveying a sea of humanity. "There are no bunks and no food," said Mick with a smile. "I've booked places on the floor; same price." The hut was mayhem. I wondered how the staff retained their sanity, let alone their obvious good humour. We ate sardines and I scrounged a bowl of coffee. At nine, the floor was swept and people bedded down on tables, on benches, even in the sink. I tried to sleep but only dozed. The room was full of mumbles and curses, scratching, and a restless anticipation of the morning.

At midnight we got up and weaved our way out between the bodies. In one place hands were held up for me to walk on – there was no floor space. Bernie had to go back to get Mike, who had failed to wake up, and his passage was marked by a sequence of incredulous French swearing. We fixed crampons, turned on torches and set off. The path was obvious, a yard deep trench in the snow behind the hut.

But soon we were spread out on the huge slope of the Dôme de Gautier.

I plodded up, pausing for a rest at each turn. Snow glittered beneath my feet in the torchlight. Down in the valley the roads looked like lava flows, ribbons of red and orange fire. The sky above was deep black and the stars brilliant; for a moment I felt that I was on a slope between heaven and hell. Far below me a cluster of torches marked the progress of the 1am starters and beyond them lights around the hut showed the next group were getting ready. I carried on upward.

Gradually the pure black of the night lightened and the bulk of the mountain became visible. It daunted me. Mick and Tony were already far ahead; Bernie's torch was a few hundred yards above and Mike and Sue were just behind. Life became a matter of placing one foot in front of another, of concentrating on moving forward. I remember thinking that this was one of the easiest routes in the Alps and feeling momentarily depressed. But then I knew it didn't matter – I was doing as much as I was able and enjoying the experience, that's what really counts.

A lone Japanese climber passed me and we grunted greetings. Bernie held a one-sided conversation with him for an hour before realising that the figure wasn't me; so much for his opinion of my conversation. The three of us reached the summit close together, shook hands and hugged each other. The summit was ours, the roof of Europe spread out before us, rows of peaks silhouetted against the orange streak of the sky. We pulled on down jackets and sat on our ropes to wait for the dawn.

ANN STEVENS

Tiptoe Through the Tuli

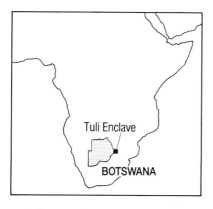

Tuli Enclave

BOTSWANA

It took the mud wasp four days to complete its home. Four days of repeated concentrated flights from the shrinking mud shores of the Limpopo – not "grey green greasy", but shallow and sluggishly brown – to the roof of our tent. The result, a smooth cone with a neat circular entry hole, hung on the hot canvas directly above my pillow. What became of it after that we never knew, for our own occupancy of the tent was over.

After a while the insect, huge though it was by our standards, had ceased to worry us. It was apparent that its interest as it droned steadily past our heads through the motionless heat was not in us, but the task in hand. Thus we co-existed peaceably and without fear. Where it went at night we never knew, for then we had the tent to ourselves. Or so we assumed! A nightly torchlight inspection of all corners before retiring was enough to reassure us into instant sleep. Rising at 4.30am and walking for hours in the African sun, in a combined mood of nervous anticipation, excitement, boredom and shameless fear, would cure the most chronic insomniac, and lull the most determined phobia about things that crawl, fly and bite. By ten o'clock every two-legged creature in the camp was comatose in blissful disregard of danger.

With six others (of assorted age and sex, though all younger than my husband and myself), we had come to the Tuli Enclave – the south-easternmost region of Botswana bordered on the south by the Limpopo River and South Africa. We were on what was described as a Wild Life Trail in which "trailists" would be given the chance to "find themselves and their limitations". This proved to be true, and we all surprised ourselves, both with our achievement and, sometimes, our failings.

We entered Botswana at Pont Drift, a tiny border crossing which proudly boasts that "it is perhaps the only international frontier where, in times of flood, travellers and luggage have to be winched across the border in a chairlift". Despite our fervent hopes of flash floods, however, the Limpopo was shrunken and sluggish and we were able to ford it in disappointingly mundane fashion. Our luggage and supplies, including six huge water melons purchased on the journey north, were piled into an open-backed truck; we clambered gamely on top of the heap, clamped our sunhats obediently on top of the lot and ground our way, in low gear and high tension, towards the mysterious wilderness on the northern bank.

Ian, our guide, was young, energetic, bush-wise – and armed! Johannes, our Botswanan co-guide and driver, was stoic and clearly wondered what all the fuss was about. This was, after all, his natural habitat. But such is the adaptability of the human animal that, after our five days in the bush, we all felt like seasoned trackers – hardened to heat and thirst, and almost blasé about the dangers that might lurk behind every bush and under each clump of grass and burning stone.

Our walks were not uneventful. A black mamba, one minute coiled ropelike round a branch, then dropping in an instant to the undergrowth, was sufficient to galvanise tired legs in all directions. Angry baboons, engaged in a violent family feud which ended in the death of a young one, resented our watchful presence and descended ferociously from the trees in barking hordes to drive us away.

A thrill of a different kind was the sight of giraffes grazing in a low golden sunset. With graceful, swaying necks, swooping and reaching, topped with placid doe eyes gazing out fearlessly beneath two furry and ineffectual pseudo-horns, their chequered hides seemed to capture and enhance the evening glow, as did the herds of grazing impala and waterbuck which nervously leapt away at our approach.

Some wonders came on a small scale. A rotating cricket ball in a hollow of the path contained a humble dung-beetle, burying in the sand the spherical nursery and larder in which to lay its eggs (these only to be eaten later by foraging baboons). Reckless, barehanded scrabbling in a scorpion's hole produced, to our great relief on Ian's behalf, not the more recent inhabitant of the nest but shards of pottery thought to be a child's burial pot. In places, the ground glittered with chips of mica and quartz, covetously collected as we passed, along with pieces of bone small enough for us to carry. The Botswana customs, however, proved exceedingly possessive over the bones, confiscating them and, presumably, tossing them back into the bush.

We didn't see a kill. We could only imagine one, on the black night drive after watching the sun set on a pride of lions lying somnolent and well fed in their secret glade where, persistently, we had hunted them out and then, reverently, left them alone.

The placid bush, stretching unbroken for numberless miles, seemed inadequate to hide the sudden death evidenced by the bleached remains fading in the pitiless sun. Sheets of yellow flowers fed on the goodness leached into the stony soil from the scattered kills. There was a special smell, particularly potent in the heat of late afternoon – a yellow-green sourness arising from grass and flowers and scrub.

Recent rains had caused foliage to flourish, and in places the grass was frighteningly concealing in its height and density. The boundless space was perversely claustrophobic in its denial of any obvious means of escape.

One memorable day a herd of several hundred elephant across our path delayed our small party for several hours in the midday heat. For a brief while, edging nearer through long grass, ducking low behind bushes too small to climb, fear turned to excitement. We were all Meryl Streep and Robert Redford, acting out the drama in front of the camera, minds already formulating the tale we would tell our friends on our return. If we did return, of course!

Meeting elephant on foot is not to be undertaken lightly. Another guide had been mauled to death, despite firing three shots – a fact for thoughtful pondering as we crouched helplessly in a sparse shrubbery, like World War I infantrymen pinned in their trench under fire which never, that day, came. Before the wind turned with the sun, the herd swung out of our path, turning back on itself in a wave of trumpeting, tearing and crashing the mopane bushes and squirting jets of muddy water. Energy was released with the tension, and we scrambled easily up a steep stony rise from which, awestruck, we gazed and gazed as the majestic, ponderous, unaware – and, after all, surely harmless – creatures continued their lives with oblivious dignity.

The arrogant male who charged our safari truck in a dry river bed was not so unaware. Incensed by our attentions to his harem, he built up an incredible speed in a short time. An elephant can move at 45kph when pressed. So, fortunately, could our four-wheel-drive vehicle – and up an almost vertical bank of loose sand and shingle. Perhaps it rose on the wings of our prayers?

That stalwart vehicle was a mixed blessing. A marvellous refuge after a five-hour walk over rough, hot ground, whose each incline was sprinkled treacherously with loose stones which unbalanced the unwary canvas-shod foot and caused eyes to be downcast, and away both from the beauty and the other hazards of the terrain. Ian, more appropriately clad in walking boots and ankle protectors, seemed on occasion to be unaware that his stumbling, cursing charges were falling further and further behind to meet with who knew what perils. To sink onto the hot wooden seats of the truck or, more adventurously, to stand charioteer-style behind the cab, was a temporary relief. But to Johannes, each swerve and tilt of the dusty track was a challenge – each pothole and low-hanging branch a hazard to be approached at speed and quickly passed. Thus, battered beneath, behind and above, arms braced on hot metal rails, exhilaration and exhaustion vied for supremacy as we raced back to camp.

Camp was safety, its line of tents firmly turned against the measureless outside, facing only the river and the sunrise. Camp was home, a primitive shower-bucket hung on a rope with chattering monkeys as an audience, hot food cooked over an open fire. It was relief after danger, rest after fatigue, cool drinks from a gas-cooled freezer, somewhere to feel proud and brave and self-fulfilled. Our party, previously unacquainted, were quickly merged by adversity, united in delights, already bound by mutual reminiscence.

Camp was also danger. On the last night a scorpion appeared by the firestones, amid bare feet spread wearily in the warm dust. Held gently but firmly by a knife blade, it obligingly sprayed its deadly venom in a demonstration of its evil intent. Then, in due reverence for all things live and wild and free, it was sent on its way in a wide, gentle arc down the river bank, out into Africa where it belonged, and we did not.

ANDREW MEERING

CROSSING BORDERS

There are few things that consistently epitomise what the travelling essence is all about more than border crossings. Suddenly you are alone and stateless. There is a degree of tension because you are about to pass from somewhere experienced into somewhere untried. It is the part of the journey where I feel most vulnerable and furthest from home.

It is that frank moment when you are distilled down to your basic denuded ingredients, a name, a number, a nationality, a free spirit and a few belongings. Where you have travelled from is in the past and where you propose to travel to will not materialise until tomorrow. The border is the point where one door closes before the next opens. It's like the point in moving house where your sticks of furniture are all out on the pavement under the gaze of passers-by. In limbo and caught in suspense until a piece of bureaucratic ritual is completed and finally the next chapter and the next country may begin, while leaving another indelible mark in the stamp collection I call a passport.

Borders are also incongruous. They stand there symbolically as the end of one thing and the beginning of something else; Capitalism back to back with Communism, Buddhism to Islam, East to West, as black and white squares on a chess board. However, when you are waiting to cross, this seldom appears evident. Most border posts lack the drama of Checkpoint Charlie.

It could be a bridge over a slow dirty river where the opposite bank is the mirror image of the very one on which you stand. There are still the same women washing clothes on boulders, drying them on rocks, the small brown children still swim, all amongst the garbage and the discarded motor tyres. It could be the unanticipated bend on a winding road around some mountain pass. A hut, three men, a striped pole, freedom beyond and a three-hundred-foot fall is all it consists of.

It could be two ends of the same street, like the time I crossed the border from Ecuador into Peru at Tumbes. Most of the street had been dug up – the drains, I believe. In the general confusion of trucks, passengers changing buses, hawkers, chickens, children kicking stones, stalls, Indians with white hats and bad teeth, a three-legged one-eyed dog, and blackmarketeers, the division in nationality had become temporarily forgotten due to the international urgency for détente on effluence. I walked right past the immigration office, located between a clothing store and a bank, before I realised I was in Peru.

I remember crossing the Brazilian border into Venezuela by the route north of Boa Vista, across the Gran Sabana. The road had brought us up from Manaus on the Amazon. We had traversed the jungle. After the claustrophobia of travelling below tree-height for two thousands kilometres with all its irritants – humidity, and insects in a stifling breezeless corridor that was no wider than the tree clearing on either side of the tracks – we emerged into the grasslands. The rolling grasslands of the Gran Sabana, savannah and occasional palms agitated by a warm wind, backdropped by an Ektachrome blue sky, were an immense release.

There is a border post, south of a town called Eldorado, which stands as an isolated shack with a wide verandah. There are no other buildings for some miles in any direction. Three men on this occasion were sitting on the verandah with typewriters, wearing T-shirts and baseball caps. We sat below them on a lawn for the best part of a day while we completed the formalities.

It was the total invisibility of anything I could conceptualise as marking the border, with the homogeneity of waving grasses in all directions, that struck me as absurd – like a canvas on which the artist has grown bored with the central theme and hastily completed the surround. The real border obviously was the end of the jungle to the south, rather than some arbitrary line drawn across a map by some absent politician. The irony of this particular incident was further illustrated by the insistence of the Brazilians on spraying both our truck and ourselves against foot and mouth disease, only to have the process repeated again by the Venezuelans. Particularly ironic as *both* countries were afflicted with foot and mouth anyway. They also made us consume our perishable foodstuffs. Too polite to confiscate the cheese and sausages, a chap with a large machete chopped everything into finger-food portions like those at a society wedding.

This year I visited "The Golden Triangle". I didn't actually know before I got to Thailand that this could be accurately located on a map. I had been under the impression that "The Golden Triangle" was no more than a loosely-contrived euphemism for assorted acts of drug trafficking, private armies and "Special Forces" bravado.

However, the area takes its name from a confluence of rivers, the Mekong and some lesser stream, at the spot where Laos, Thailand and Burma rub shoulders. I was rather hoping it would boast at least a small element of excitement, if not danger. In fact the place, when viewed from a ramshackle restaurant sited to overlook a sandbank strategically placed in the middle of the Mekong, was quite tranquil. It could have been the location for some Asian regatta.

At one stage a few Laotian buddhist priests took a swim from the far shore, but it had the calm that goes with obscurity – strange for a river which, not too far downstream, had been a killing ground for American, Vietnamese, Thai and Laotian, let alone the meeting point for the political extremes of the three neighbours.

An ancient patrol boat chugged downstream in the early evening. At dawn the next day Laotian/Vietnamese propaganda was broadcast through a loudhailer from the opposite bank. It could have been Reveille at Butlin's. The tinny, shrill proclamations came through thick swirling river mist. I doubt whether the broadcaster would have had the same courage in broad daylight.

Border crossings, like police checks, always make me a little nervous.

"Su passaporte, por favor."

Why me, why pick on me? There are six waiting in the line. What have I done wrong? Where in this ritual have I violated a subtle but required ground rule? Suddenly there appear a thousand things I have neglected. The official (Pablo) in the ill-fitting uniform pauses (so does Juan his sidekick, understudy and bootlicker). Whatever it is I have done, it is surely incredible or at least it is to him. I can guess. It is the documentation. He has never seen such documentation. Surely in the name of Santa Maria this must be the bureaucracy of the former bourgeois running dogs. Do I not know that the glorious republic has revolutionised everything, including visa applications?

Or is it the photograph that shows a mild-mannered clerk with the pale, sober features of one who spends little time in the sun. The character here is dusty with ten days' stubble and has clearly been on the road for nearly a millennium. Driven to flight by some dark-eyed Latin lover, he is now compelled to roam confined in the lyrics of some sad ballad, with one too many mornings and a thousand miles behind.

Worse, the numbers of her Britannic Majesty's subjects have by pure chance been thrown up by random number on the yellowed report on computer listing in his hands. This is the gringo marxist "Shining Path" sympathiser from Lima. This is the man to be held for routine questioning. This is the man with six keys of cocaine. This is the man shortly to be held incommunicado. To be dragged into the ante-room away from the observation of others. To be stripped, frisked, have the lining torn from his baggage, legs spread, palms against the concrete wall. The toothpaste wrung from the tube and his belongings piled like the debris of a molested carcass in the centre of the floor . . .

The passport is returned and momentarily the official's face breaks into something like a smile. A lull in diplomatic relations, though only for an instant.

"Welcome, *señor*."

All is forgiven. I have been adopted. I am with my new friends. I am across the border.

FRANK GARDNER

ON AND OFF THE BALKAN EXPRESS

The demise of the old Orient Express to the East, although sad, has not put an end to either rail travel in the Balkans or the romance that this inspires, travelling second class through a countryside that has changed little since the time of Agatha Christie's epic *Murder on the Orient Express.*

Prompted perhaps by the rosy posters on the London Underground, we boarded a train at Victoria one July afternoon, bound for Bulgaria – a country that usually escapes the attentions of the world's press and of which we ourselves were shamefully ignorant.

Relishing the prospect of the two-and-a-half day train journey as the best possible way to reach a country, we climbed onto an orange TGV in Paris – one of these carrot-shaped *Train Grande Vitesse* expresses that are supposed to hurtle you across the Continent at 168mph. French Railways have got comfort down to a fine art, and at midnight we eased off so smoothly that we were well clear of the station before anyone realised we were moving.

We awoke in Switzerland, craning our necks through the window to watch Alpine crags float past, their peaks dusted with July snow. Racing through the valleys we passed clean, wooden-slatted farms surrounded by vineyards and neat chalets that crept up the mountainside like a besieging army. The Simplon Tunnel. For twenty minutes we rattled through it at speed, emerging into another country where the seriousness of Swiss architecture gave way to the rust-coloured roofs and flaking stucco walls of Italy.

Milano Centrale. A mesh of overhead cables led into the echoing cavern of the station. A train driver leaned out of his window and beamed at us, a go-faster turtle transfer pasted onto the side of his cab. Trieste. Sunburned arms leaned out of windows as we rounded the sweeping expanse of the Adriatic riviera, its sunlit bays teeming with yachts, the pink villas hiding behind hedges of pines, and puffy clouds building up over the Istrian Peninsular, across the water in Yugoslavia.

We joined the Istanbul Express, mingling with a small army of homebound Turkish guestworkers, picking our way over barricades of bulging packing cases and catching our first whiff of the famous Balkan tobacco.

Belgrade. In the muggy heat of mid-morning the station appeared to be almost swimming. Fat Serbian women sat about on trolleys, resting their scarved heads on bulging forearms. Blue-uniformed porters, apparently little interested in the day's business, lounged in a circle, pushing their military caps back on their glistening foreheads. A posse of Yugoslav soldiers strolled past, dressed in colourful uniforms of white cross-straps, tilted sidecaps and buckled boots. Two gypsy girls, very dark, lay wrapped around each other on a bed of newspapers, surrounded by the detritus of their breakfast.

Heading south, the tractors gave way to horses and carts, bereted men tossed hay into stooks and women wielded huge scythes. The track ran alongside green rivers where families swam and fished. Tiny station halts flashed past, the solitary official waving a red flag and the clanging bell growing fainter down the line.

Dimitrovgrad, the Yugoslav border village. Cicadas hummed outside in the still afternoon while burly customs men walked the corridors, asking questions and searching luggage. We trundled gently into Bulgaria, entering a flat and unexciting landscape. A castle hove into view, grey and mysterious, then turned out to be a derelict factory. Sofia, the capital, began suddenly, only forty minutes from the border, the crumbling tiled cottages merging into the high-rise apartment blocks, the village dovetailing into the city.

Sofia Central Station: a concrete monstrosity, so forbidding in the twilight that it was sorely tempting to carry on to Turkey. We walked into a vast hall with space-age lights way up on the distant ceiling and promptly lost ourselves amidst Cyrillic timetables, crowds, soldiers and overloud announcements. Outside the night was warm and people sat around a statue to Socialist Achievement, smoking and talking quietly as if awaiting some bad news.

We passed a mosque – the "Banja Bashi" – then a Greek Orthodox church, but failed to find a restaurant still open at 10pm. The Bulgarians are frugal, to say the least, with their street lighting, so we narrowly missed blundering into other pedestrians in the dark. At a café we ordered two orange juices with nuts, unaware that due to the official exchange rate that was to cost us seven pounds (four pounds for a saucer of peanuts).

Four floors above Marshal Tolbuhin Boulevard our room looked out over the clanking trams on one side and a bullet-scarred courtyard on the other. Later in the night a deafening storm broke out, with rain lashing the tiles and thunder rebounding off the encircling mountains.

Sofia proved to be an attractive, open-air place, rich in onion-domed churches, parks, fountains, cafés and vendors of ice-cream and icons. Our enjoyment was curtailed, however, when we came up against the full weight of Comecon bureaucracy at its historic best: Bulgarian currency regulations. At the *bureau de change* ("Speak only Russian or Bulgarian. Next . . ."), a notice reminds you that all hotel bills are to be paid in hard currency. Our hotel insisted on local lev. We offered them lev so they asked for our official exchange paper. "No. This is Change Paper No.3. You must give Change Paper No.4." Back to the *bureau de change*. "Impossible to change money without border entry cards." But these the hotel would not return to us until we had paid our bill – in lev. And so on.

After the stultifying food queues and dour faces of the capital, the Rila Monastery was a breath of fresh air. The dawn bus drove south through forested hills where the golden domes of churches loomed out of the mist, reflecting the morning sun. Village houses were low-roofed, half-timbered and covered in vines. Necklaces of drying tobacco hung across the walls and in the dusty streets moustachioed Bulgars led donkeys, weighed down with wicker panniers, and eyed the bus with suspicion.

Three-and-a-half thousand feet up in the mountains, Rilski Manastir, as it is known locally, has survived for a thousand years as a remote sanctuary and object of pilgrimage for those coming to donate gold in the hope of curing terminally ill relatives. This gold now decorates chapel frescoes which graphically depict hairy demons tempting saints, then roasting alive in hellfire. In the inner courtyard stone fountains spouted ice-cold water from the mountain, stags' antlers crowned the entrance hall and carved wooden balconies rose one above the other, sandwiched between chessboard pattern walls, arranged mesmerically like an optical illusion.

On the cobbled stones elderly monks with blue velvet hats and plaited grey hair chatted to an immensely fat *babushchka* who guarded the lavatories. A bakery nearby produced powdery loaves still hot from the oven while a café sold *plodov sok* – peach nectar – by the cupful. There was a momentary flurry of activity when a party of high-ranking Soviet officers was shown round, flanked by official photographers; then the monastery returned to the soporific calm of a Balkan afternoon.

As we returned to Sofia the rainclouds emptied onto a desolate collective farm by the roadside, polishing the rusting machinery and pouring down the red posters advertising the forthcoming thirteenth Congress of the BKP – the Bulgarian Communist Party. Sofia was rather attractive in the rain, which was more than could be said for our "traditional Bulgarian folkloric meal" that evening: peppered dumplings and something with the remains of tubes still protruding from it. ("Bulgarian food is very delicious," enthused our official guidebook).

We left Bulgaria, in due course, by one of the most dramatic of all

Styles apart in Bulgaria.
ABOVE: The Rila Monastery, a mountain sanctuary for pilgrims and tourists.
BELOW: State propaganda in the capital, Sofia.
(On and Off the Balkan Express)

LEFT: Lobster terminé, Caribbean-style. *(Taking a Dive)*
RIGHT: 'Gingerbread house' at Chautauqua. *(A Sack Tied in the Middle)*

A room with a view. *(The Mysteries of Mindos)*

the Eastern European borders: the Dragoman Pass. With a long and mournful whistle the train entered the pass at Slivnitsa and picked up speed. Rusted Cyrillic signposts lay broken by the track as we curved through rugged outcrops, descending all the time into the plains of Yugoslavia. With another eery whistle the locomotive trundled across a girder bridge and the ground fell away beneath us as we traversed a boulder-strewn gorge. We passed a Bulgarian machine-gun post, then a ploughed strip, barbed wire and arc lamps – the border – and suddenly we were in Yugoslavia.

We headed straight for a restaurant.

TAKING A DIVE

From the light aircraft tossing unsteadily on the heatwaves, Anagarda looked the antithesis of all that is expected of Caribbean islands. Even from the air it could be seen only at very close range, its highest point being a mere twenty feet. Directly above it, as if captured on X-ray, its constitution became apparent: spanning from it in all directions just below the surface of the translucent waters, the skeleton of the third largest and arguably the most dangerous barrier reef in the world.

The treacherous nature of these waters seems in the past to have attracted occupants of like compulsion: only men who understood the deception could survive on the island; only those who could turn the destruction of others to their own advantage could profit from living there. On even the calmest of nights, cargo ships from Europe would glide towards the inviting lights and the mercy of the pirates. Today Anagarda still exists like the single exposed knuckle of a sleeping Scylla.

We landed on a chalky airstrip to the north of the island. From ground level the terrain seemed no more hospitable – the treeless, dry scrubland unalleviated by shadow or undulation, the only substantial shelter offered by a shack superimposed on ground near the runway. Here a small group of people waited to receive relatives or to catch the plane themselves for shopping in Tortola. The familiar sound of reggae limping from a radio in a nearby truck seemed to accentuate rather than alleviate the isolation of this West Indian wasteland.

We stepped forward to the only other car, which we presumed was from the hotel, and introduced ourselves. "I think you're expecting us," said Charlie into the window. After a moment the driver got out and with an almost reluctant smile offered us the back seat. As we trundled down the scarred road in silence I began to long for the radio in the other truck.

"How far is the hotel?"

"At least thirty miles," he said, and looked back smiling in the mirror to see our reaction. I smiled back and he looked away. About six minutes later we were driving through the gates of the hotel.

It was a small open building with a row of rooms leading off it parallel to the sea a few yards away. A handful of stunted palms and a couple of brightly flowering shrubs distinguished the area from the surrounding scrub. It soon became apparent that there was no-one else in the hotel.

Sitting alone that evening at the bar outside, we asked to book a dive for the next morning. "You can't go diving here now," said the man without looking at us. "It's too late notice."

"But we've come here specially for the diving," said Charlie insistently. "In all the guidebooks it says you specialise in taking divers onto the wrecks here. If you can't do it, we might as well go back now to Tortola."

"You can't do that," he retorted. "There's no plane until the day after tomorrow." Smiling triumphantly, he turned away as if the conversation were over. After a moment Charlie tried again: "Well, you must have an air compressor here. I don't see the difficulty. We could easily fill the tanks for tomorrow."

The response was abrupt and in a tone of mock subservience: "O.K. If you want to dive, then you must. Tomorrow, ten o'clock," and walked angrily away.

There was hardly a beach to speak of, just a narrow strip of coarse sand and coral where the sea stroked tirelessly at this errant piece of reef that so stubbornly refused to return to its place under water. We decided to walk along it, at least out of range of the hotel, to watch the sunset. But the evening rays did little to dispel the uneasiness that was fast accumulating. As we walked, the tiny fingers of coral flicked away from our feet. Pieces of white, sand-blasted driftwood stuck out of the sand like exposed limbs from a shallow grave. Later Charlie said of that walk that it was as if you could feel all around you the untold deaths and all the shipwrecks still out there. Yet at the time even he had felt too subdued to mention it.

In the morning our captain seemed more animated. His joviality, although consistently at our expense, was at least preferable to the determined aggression of the evening before. We searched through the cardboard boxes in the shop for acceptable masks and snorkels, found fins vaguely the right size and took them to the pier. The gear assembled there resembled equipment used in old sixties movies – the life-vests were more like those taken on planes, and far less effective, since the automatic inflators were now useless and we had to rely on being able to inflate them by mouth. The diaphragms and mouthpieces of the regulators were old and decayed; and yet, somehow, the equipment we sorted out eventually satisfied us sufficiently to continue. Moreover, we were, by now, too involved in this game of wills to back down.

We spun off at a frightening speed, clinging on just to stay inside the boat. Beneath us raced the blurred shapes of the reef only inches below the bows. As the captain swerved to avoid a jutting rock or turned to chase a shark through the shallows, the tanks clanked frantically in the back and the masks skimmed across the floor. We headed for open sea.

It was one of those days, so typical of the summer months in the Caribbean, when clouds stream continuously across the sun, sending dense, giant shadows gliding over the sea. As the waves mounted to a ten-foot swell, their effortless movement seemed to mock the struggles of our tiny speedboat. We stalled. As the captain was tinkering with the engine we asked why we were not diving in calmer waters nearer the hotel – after all, there were allegedly more than six hundred wrecks to choose from. He did not answer.

"I hope you can find your own way back again!" he said eventually, laughing, touching on our very thoughts. Charlie looked seriously worried for the first time; I began to feel sick.

The engine started eventually and we continued, defiantly battling with the swell, beyond sight of any island. At last we dropped anchor. "Where are we?" I asked, trying to keep my voice, and my stomach, steady. He crossed to the other side of the boat and pointed. "Down there are the boilers."

"What sort of ship is it?" I asked.

"You'll find out."

Angry and scared, I was feeling far too nauseous to retaliate. Neither would I have dared dive in such conditions with someone so determined to unnerve, had I not been so desperate to assuage my sea-sickness. There was no alternative now. We tumbled over the side towards the sunken ship.

Even near the sea-bed, the swell was so strong that following him was a struggle: as we closed in upon the side of the wreck it became a fight to resist being dashed against it. Beneath a shelf on the hull I saw the captain had found a lobster. He caught it, and in a flurry of sand dragged it away from its lair. It was a blue-black female carrying her eggs protected under her abdomen. As she struggled, the eggs began to fall. She slipped away and darted for the rocks. He snatched after her but caught only a leg, which snapped noiselessly in his hand.

I floated on behind him as senseless as a drunk. Suddenly he pointed to the sea-bed. Beneath me, drifting across the sand with the flow of the current, rolled a thousand bones. Despite the feeling of rising panic, I fought to remain clear-headed: I would not think what I knew he wanted me to believe. These had to be goats or sheep or cows, nothing more. The captain motioned to me and, picking up two bones, demonstrated the movement of the ball and socket, and pointed to my elbow. I tried to focus instead on the sea-bed to find some evidence of an animal cargo, some indication that my own imagination was at fault. When I turned towards Charlie he was looking ahead at the prow of the ship; there, silhouetted against the open water, stood the gallows, leaning slightly to one side, and from them, still intact, dangled a noose. The captain, holding it close to his neck was swinging suspended in the swell like a corpse.

By the time we came to leave the island, Charlie had convinced me that the ship had sunk with animals on board: the skull he had found bore no resemblance to a man's – the shape of the head was elongated and the jaw protruded like that of a goat; surely the living quarters had been too small and close to the engine-room, and anyway hadn't slavery been abolished long before the era of the steamship? All the same, as we arrived at the airport, I could not resist asking the captain for his own macabre explanation.

"Ah!" he said. "That was a Greek merchant ship. It went down with all lives on board. They were Arawaks being taken back as slaves. Funny people, them – they used to bind their children's heads to make them grow lengthways. Yes. Funny people with funny heads." He laughed. "As good as animals. Anyway, what doesn't matter to anyone else doesn't matter to me."

JUDITH TAYLOR

A SACK TIED IN THE MIDDLE

Reaching Chautauqua is easier than learning how to spell it. People Express runs a quick and efficient service from Newark to Buffalo. It is also cheap, so no-one minds walking across the tarmac and climbing the metal steps to the plane. A cash register is trundled down the aisle while the steward collects our fares. There's hardly time to buy and drink a coffee and eat my Sara Lee cellophane-sealed danish before my plane lands. The journey by car from the airport promises to be smooth and uneventful, once I'm accustomed to traffic on the wrong side of the road.

The Niagara region is wine-growing country. Neat rows of vines fill the fields on either side of the road. Everything is pleasantly rural. The vineyards give way to woods and trees, and soon the smooth shimmer of Lake Erie can be seen. I want to call it the sea as it stretches to the horizon. The northern shore is actually in Canada. Sailing the Great Lakes can be more dangerous than crossing the Atlantic, due to the sudden storms which blow up from nowhere.

Turning south from Lake Erie, we begin a long, steady climb to Westfield and Mayville. White wooden houses and farms edge the road. Everything seems very spread out; there's such a lot of room to sprawl in here. Even the small towns are spacious. There are no garden fences or hedges, but tall shady trees and sweeping green lawns. Many homes fly an American flag in the garden. I inquire if it's some special national commemorative day.

"No," comes the reply, "we're just very proud of our country and our flag. It's funny how visitors always notice and remark on them but wait until the 4th of July – then you'll really see flags. Don't people in England fly the Union Jack in their gardens?"

Americans have a reverence for their historic houses. If necessary they are towed from one site to another. This usually takes place in the middle of the night, the only time that the phone company will agree to unhook the low roadside telephone wires, allowing the house to be launched into the street. A confrontation with a travelling house at the dead of night must be a rather supernatural experience.

Just outside Westfield comes the first view of Chautauqua Lake. Chautauqua, the American Institution, lies halfway along the western side of the top portion of the lake. From Westfield to Mayville is no distance at all, and the road used to end there. Today Mayville is full of roadworks, making me think of the Minneapolian quip: "We have two seasons here – winter and roadbuilding." The summers are hot but the winters bring deep frost and enough snow for good skiing. Free of the roadworks we pass the Mayfly, a white-painted, stern-wheel paddle-steamer which daily plies the lake on sightseeing voyages. The old way to reach Chautauqua was to go by train to Westfield and then take a steamer into Chautauqua. A more romantic approach than the prosaic road affords today as it travels steadily through the uneventful trees and fields.

This is market garden country with wayside stalls selling fruit, flowers and vegetables, but not quite what you'd find in the Vale of Evesham. There are peaches, plums and nectarines, eggplants, zucchini, black raspberries, huge beefsteak tomatoes, squash and several varieties of melon. Produce is sold by the basket or the punnet – the small thin woven wooden boxes which strawberries in England used to come in before the arrival of cardboard and plastic ones.

Suddenly there's a sign. "Welcome to Chautauqua An American Institution" proclaims the freshly painted navy and white billboard. As we drive to the main gate I glance through the high wire fence and see lots of little wooden huts scattered among the trees. I puzzle at their purpose. Later I discover that they are private practice huts for aspiring singers and musicians.

The main entrance is through a kind of car-port with barriers next to a brick and stone building with neo-classical columns. These are adorned with hanging baskets from which spill geraniums of white, pink, crimson, mauve and peach; trailing ivy; brightly-coloured petunias; white alyssum and blue lobelia. Young, fresh-faced college students inspect our gate passes. The barrier is raised and we drive in under the portico; visitors on foot file in though the turnstile.

Pedestrians have right of way in the grounds at Chautauqua. Many visitors own or hire bicycles or tricycles of various ages and standards of efficiency. Others ride the blue-and-white canopied electric trolleys. These carry about a dozen passengers and will stop wherever they are hailed. There are also two bus routes for the east and west halves of the grounds, covered by a blue version of the bright yellow American school bus.

My first impression of Chautauqua is of trees and wooden houses, always picturesque but often packed closely together. Walking along the old worn paths of the original brickwalks, I can see the individual character of each house revealed. Many have wide porches and verandahs complete with rocking chairs or swings. Progress along these paths is slow, for there are always friends and acquaintances to stop and chat with, and frequent invitations to linger awhile and drink an iced tea on someone's front porch. Some houses have shutters and even window boxes filled with flowers. My favourite house is the exquisitely tiny, pink and white gingerbread house with the wooden lace trimming the gables.

Scattered among the houses are chapels serving many religious denominations. One night I saw a black and white cat stroll casually into one chapel, just in time for the evening service. I wonder if he managed to try them all? Chautauqua even boasts a building like a Greek temple, the open sides allowing breezes to refresh those listening to the lectures inside. Judith Thurman held us entranced as she spoke of the making of the film *Out of Africa,* and told us what Robert Redford was *really* like.

The President of Chautauqua's home on the lake shore is a pretty shade of pink. His porch is hung with tastefully co-ordinated baskets of white and pink geraniums. A large number of homes are graced with such baskets, and huge pots of flowers on their steps or verandahs, as few have gardens of any size. The exception is a ninety-two-year-old woman, Miss Smith, whose garden is across the road from her house. It has roses, delphiniums, hollyhocks, lupins, daisies, marigolds, peonies and stocks, fringed by trees and shrubs. With its wide, shallow steps and terrace it looks as though it might have floated in from eighteenth-century England.

The focal point for Chautauquans is the central plaza and amphitheatre. The carved stone fountain in the middle of the plaza is surrounded by grass dotted with seats for meetings, picnics, a place for Amish girls to work at their sewing or even doze in the sunshine, watching the world go by. The redbrick library stands at one end, the colonnade of shops at the other. To one side is the imposing Post Office building with its basement bookstore. Here a brass-fronted box with a combination lock may be rented to receive your mail. There are no postmen at Chautauqua to deliver to private homes. If you don't wish to rent a box you ask for your mail from the neatly uniformed Post Office clerks.

The amphitheatre – a wooden structure in a hollow, with air-conditioning courtesy of the open sides – seats two thousand. A roof protects the audience in wet weather. The seats are wooden and best experienced through a cushion. Here are held the Sunday services. Taking a collection from such a huge congregation assumes the proportions of a military campaign. Thank goodness they've chosen a nice long hymn to accompany the operation. Suits, unseen the rest of the week, are retrieved from closets, shoes are shined and the usual shorts and sandals discarded for an hour or two.

A gate pass entitles you to free entrance to events in the amphitheatre. Boogie with Blood, Sweat and Tears. Bop with The Monkees. Be wowed by Ferrante and Teicher's piano duets, silenced only momentarily by the wind and rain which swept through the auditorium during one memorable storm. There are regular symphony concerts; ballet and opera students also perform. Because admission is free once you have a gate pass, the audiences are large and varied. Three generations of a family come to see entertainers like Peter, Paul and Mary. Mary Travers proclaims, "My mother said we'd never last!" Yet here they are and Mary, now a proud grandmother, shows the audience a poster-sized photograph of her granddaughter.

Weeks at Chautauqua pass as days. There's so much to do and see. Leaving is hard. I wake half an hour before my alarm rouses me and I see the warm reds of the sunrise. Never again will I need my gate pass to go in or out of the grounds. As my plane circles above the lake I glance down and see its whole shape at once. Now I understand why the Indians called the lake Chautauqua: a sack tied in the middle.

ELIZABETH SYRETT

The Mysteries of Mindos

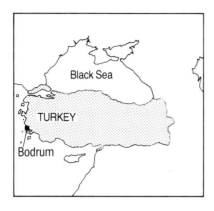

I don't know what the Turkish village of Gumushluk is like in winter, or even in the intense heat of midsummer; but in September it is magical.

In the clear water, sea creatures sway to the exotic wail of Turkish music. The sun transforms every tiny ripple on the surface of the water into a shimmering diamond, and carves a straight golden pathway to hazy Greek islands on the far horizon.

It is easy to be brave in the buoyant waters of the sheltered bay, and with unaccustomed ease one swims on and on along this heavenly highway.

Of course if you prefer to get no more than your feet wet, you can wade out to a less distant island inhabited only by rabbits. Some are discreetly camouflaged in grey or beige; others defy the laws of survival in bold black or conspicuous white – all are equally sleek and fit, and are today rejoicing in a gift of watermelon.

The village itself is small and pretty and neatly concentrated around the water's edge. It is comprised largely – but not entirely – of restaurants. There are a couple of "general stores", a carpet shop, one or two cafés where the local men play cards and backgammon, a number of extremely beautiful summer homes where rich Turkish families take refuge from the cities; also a few simple houses of the sort where an old man and his wife can be seen eating dinner cross-legged on the floor – and high above beach, harbour and houses is a mosque, its slender minaret surveying all village activity.

This peninsula is the site of the ancient Greek city of Mindos, of which no more remains than the great stone blocks clearly visible beneath the surface of the water. Its great legacy is not forgotten and two small hotels bear the noble name of "Mindos". However, if one intends to travel by dolmas, they must master the modern Turkish name, "Gumushluk".

Most likely you will want to visit Bodrum (half-an-hour and 35p away) to shop for Turkish delight (delicious) or Turkish trousers (much worn by local women, but distinctly unflattering) or the ubiquitous crocheted suede waistcoats for five pounds or less – and most importantly to see Bodrum's Crusader castle with its excellent museum. In particular the tower devoted to a clever and imaginative display of antique glass, and the English tower where one may take a glass of wine in a baronial hall with fine views of the sea.

Also, you might care to see one of the Seven Wonders of the Ancient World. On an obscure residential street not far from the bus station, are the remains of *the original* mausoleum, built in 350BC for King Mausolus by his widow. It is surely worth a ten-minute detour to visit what has been left by time and vandals, of a great structure which has given a word to our language – and which few of us supposed still to exist.

It is much hotter in Bodrum, and despite its attractions one soon tires of busy streets (even if there *are* camel trains amongst the traffic) and longs for the gentle breezes of Gumushluk. Ancient Mindos slipped beneath the sea, alive again to bring solace to the soul – and the body as well.

There are all those restaurants (at least sixteen of them) ready to serve good, inexpensive food at almost any hour. Starting with the traditional breakfast – a glass of clear tea, bread and butter, curd cheese, black olives and pale delicately clover-scented honey, served on a metal tray like an Indian *thali*.

For lunch, share a few salad dishes and some *borek* (cheese pastries) accompanied by a bottle of soothing red wine – preceded perhaps by the excellent fish soup – and followed of course by Turkish coffee. The bill for two people will be between three and four pounds (depending on whether the fish soup is available).

For the remainder of the afternoon the management have provided thick straw mats for sun-bathing on the beach in front of their establishment, or comfortable chairs in the shade of a tamarisk tree.

Paradise at little cost is always so much more satisfying than the millionaire's version. Ideally paradise should be a gift rather than a purchase.

The bay is a perfect crescent shape, and later when the moon rises, it too, by coincidence, echoes the Turkish symbol.

Now it is time to dine more elegantly. We will spend seven, maybe eight pounds for two. Not because the dishes are any more expensive at the place which is best and most popular, but because at dinner we will have, in addition, meat or some modest sea-food (as everywhere in the Mediterranean, fish is scarce and relatively expensive). We will take our coffee and brandy upstairs, seated on a soft sofa before a window that is open to the warm, still night air. Turkish brandy tastes quite good when a generous measure is served in a large balloon glass – and the view is of bright stars and dark sea. The grand yachts have moored cosily for the night, but the eager fishing boats are just setting out in pursuit of those elusive red mullet and swordfish, squid and octopus.

We are in a dream as we stroll back to our curious little hotel. It is old and traditional in style and could quite easily be charming if anyone ever bothered to clean it. Our brown-shuttered windows open right out over the water and, but for the bobbing orange peel and the knowledge that this is the precise spot where the waiter guts and scales the fish we could jump straight out of the window into the sea. One day I probably will anyway.

Inside, our room is very white and very bare. In one corner a lacy fretwork of cobwebs descends from the high ceiling to the tiled floor – always lightly covered in sand. There are four built-in shelves and some hooks for our clothing, a quite adequate lamp and two reasonably clean beds. It is austere but not unacceptable.

The bathroom however is *far* from acceptable, although strangely the "en suite" bathroom is a feature in which the owner takes great pride. Bath mats, towels, lavatory paper are unknown. There is no mirror, no shelf, no plug. Water comes (sometimes) from a crude tap. The walls are cracked and peeling, the shower a thing of dread. The water heater is mounted on the wall at an alarming angle, and the large and frightening gas cylinder is obliged to sit on a wooden chair in order to reach the pipe which is several feet too short. The concrete floor is always awash. As is so often the case with primitive plumbing, there is water everywhere except where you want it.

Still, it is much improved since my husband made some emergency repairs, and now we have a plastic bucket so that when the cistern is empty we can at least fetch water from the sea. And in the whitewashed courtyard outside our door, there are vines and flowers and an old lobster pot, and two heavy wooden lounging beds (only slightly broken) where tomorrow morning I will lie in the sun and finish the book I am reading.

It is true that once you have seen the rabbits and the ruins there isn't much to do in Gumushluk – but it is an excellent place to do it.

DEREK WILLIAMS

DAYS OF WINE AND CROSSES

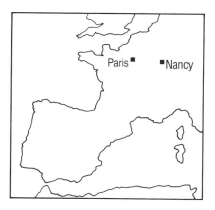

With a knowledge of Lorraine beginning and ending with Quiche and Cross, the prospect of a week in Nancy promised at least to extend my knowledge of Eastern France. Not a tourist-trap at any time of year, I thought – and this was November.

My base, a student hall of residence seemingly inhabited mainly by South Americans and North Africans, proved conveniently central. Within a day I could recognise a *pain au chocolat* at a dozen paces and realised that the bona fide *Quiche Lorraine* is really just a bacon and egg tart. Even the macaroons looked suspiciously similar to the factory versions back home, though they were born and bred in Nancy. There's a street named after them – or rather after the nuns who perfected them back in the eighteenth century for a Mother Superior of delicate constitution. Like all French hand-made biscuits and chocolates, their price is not for those with delicate purses either.

As I'm not into Art Nouveau, the building exteriors, fine though they undoubtedly are, left me cold. As my friend had a car, we spent most afternoons on excursions into the countryside.

Lorraine is noted for its fruit liqueurs: colourless, in tall, very slim bottles and extremely expensive. One fruit, the mirabelle, originates from orchards of stunted trees which line the road on the way to Verdun. One can take in the odd military cemetery en route, most notably the American one at St. Mihiel, where lie those who fell during the offensive of 1918. Verdun itself is worth a visit, with its impressive set of steps leading up to a monument. But it is the battlefield which sends a chastening tingle down the spine.

The site is reminiscent of a Forestry Commission plantation – a perfect spot for a Sunday afternoon picnic among the pines. Yet within are the remains of the three villages which were literally blown to bits one day in 1916. Arriving too late to see the museum, we drove up to the memorial, whose oblong form surveys the scenes of carnage like some wise uncle whose advice was never followed. The least one can think is that the dead have been laid out with due reverence, in perfect rows of Christian and Islamic headstones. But it's only half the story. So easy to miss, through windows at waist level around the memorial building, are piles of unidentified remains. "Surely not the real thing?" was my response, seventy years on. This happens only in remote countries of South East Asia. A drive up to the fort and the trenches brought home the more conventional picture: mud, cold and gun positions surmounted by iron domes of such a size it's a wonder they were ever hauled into position. No, they didn't pass, but would the suffering have been less if they had?

Resolution of an earlier and more personal kind has its origins in the quiet village of Domremy-la-Pucelle, birth-place of France's most famous daughter. The house itself, fossilised in the year 1420, gives some indication of why Jeanne forsook its draughty homeliness to lead her country against the English invaders.

A refreshing simplicity pervades the place: a small one-room museum depicts Jeanne's life and traces her legend, which surprisingly took off only in the 1800s. It was a relief to see no leanings towards modern technology. Yet respect is combined with a lighter touch. The visitors' book made interesting reading: "One of the enemy visited this place. Sunderland, England." And some people take full advantage of Jeanne's belated canonisation: "For success in my exam, pray for me." As one who must have inspired myriad exam questions, Jeanne must feel under no small obligation.

Such places are not to be shrugged off easily, so we headed east to Strasbourg the next day, for a change of scene and atmosphere. Taking the road south and keeping within France, we eventually encountered a signposted trail which meanders along the slope of the Vosges, cunningly taking in a succession of villages devoted to the grape: the Route du Vin. It would be a treat at any time of the year: snow in winter, aglow with new growth in spring, sleepy in summer and autumn . . . What could be more palate-quickening than to see those grapes being picked, a squeeze away from next year's drinking.

For those who can't tell a vine from a runner bean, the man-sized green bottles on village corners might offer a hint at the nature of the principal industry. We were too late for the harvest and the vines, many already pruned, held only a few remains of former glories. We made a brief stop, which was barely justified for this hopeful scrumper.

The village offered too much in the way of attractions, all crying out to be walked in, not driven through. Hopelessly romantic, with names delivering all they promise – Riquewihr, Obernai, Ribeauville – and absurdly picturesque, posing for the opening to Pinocchio. The Germanic influence is obvious, considering that Alsace was under German occupation from 1870 to 1918 and again from 1939 to 1945. Franz and Karl abound on shops and auberges. How has the region, so conveniently-sited for Prussian designs westwards, retained a sixteenth-century flavour in every one of these Vosgian gems?

A mystery I couldn't explain, in contrast to the delights of the famous Alsatian wines, whose freshness, youth and vitality offer few subtleties but much drinking pleasure. The slim, green, tapering bottles bear the names of the grape varieties: Traminer, Pinot, Sylvaner, Muscat and, most typically, Riesling. All are dry and white (except the rosé Pinot Noir), ideal chilled as an aperitif.

With vintners' signs inviting free tastings, we finally stopped in St. Hippolyte and sampled a selection of wines amid a cloud of fruit flies, a result of the mild weather. No matter; who'd begrudge a mere insect its fill? No teat pipettes here – generous glasses make bountiful sales, though not in my case. I settled for two bottles, ferry in mind.

"What makes a special wine?" I asked, when told that '85 and '83 were outstanding years. "Sun," said the woman.

A few miles further south, it's impossible to wander around Riquewihr with its celebrated Rieslings, medieval walls, tiny shuttered windows, wells and cobbled streets, without wondering how it is so well-preserved in the face of such an onslaught of wine-hungry tourists. Perhaps it's *because* of the visitors, who all contribute to its continuing prosperity.

Another famous name is connected with Kaysersberg, whose Protestant church is the birthplace of Albert Schweitzer. His sacrifice of a brilliant career for the rigours of Central Africa is all the more remarkable. Had Kaysersberg been my birthplace I'd have felt the need to return to it once a year, at least. Was this simply the enthusiasm of the first-time visitor? It may get snowed in during the winter and, once you've seen one vineyard . . . I doubt it. Narrow streets, genuine market-squares and the strange Alsatian dialect all add up to somewhere very special.

As for food, the Alsatians like giving their geese cirrhosis, but being an objector to the ethics of *foie gras* I had to try the local delicacy – the *Bäckeoffe,* a casserole of lamb, pork and beef marinated in Riesling and topped with carrots and potatoes. Enough to satisfy anyone's craving for meat, even if it's really only a hot-pot. Even in the modest restaurant we chose, a family party of a dozen went through the card, culminating in enormous meringue sundaes. Clearly, when the sun shines, the money flows. Somehow I can't imagine a hunger march passing through the *Route du Vin,* but it would make an interesting choice. With a few glasses of Muscat, even the driest baguette would acquire a life of its own.

GEORGINA CARRINGTON

Art Exhibition

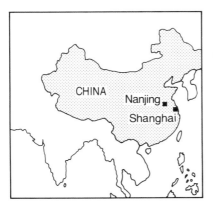

The tourist coaches disgorge their contents into the forecourt of the Jinling Hotel, Nanjing. The colours and shapes of middle-class Europe, America, Japan, Australia, stream through plate glass doors and stand in dazed clusters among their luggage, whilst tour leaders complete yet another set of check-in formalities.

Polished chrome and marble reflect luxuriant indoor gardens. A pianist's vacuous tinkling drifts from the intercommunication system. It could be the foyer of an international hotel anywhere in the world.

Outside, late autumn sunshine filters through the industrial haze. A complex of fountains makes dark splashes on patterned paving. The white-painted concrete fence marks a boundary, on the far side of which the other China, in sober-suited rows, peers with impassive curiosity at this world within their world, as we stand before cages at a zoo. We are aware of another China. It flows past endlessly on jangling bicycles; it smiles from doorways and factory workbenches when we are shown round. But in the restaurants we are segregated; even our Chinese guides eat separately. We shop in Friendship Stores for tourists, where they speak English. The other China is always just beyond reach.

Mary's padlock had broken, and she needed a replacement before we moved on tomorrow. Reception couldn't help. Neither could the girls in the hotel arcade, with its jade, cloisonné and mirror-smoothe laquerwork, all bargains to the wealthy. So I sketched a padlock on an envelope, and three of us ventured into the streets.

China goes to bed early. At 8.30pm the cyclists were thinning out and shops were closing, but delicious smells wafted from the stalls selling hot snacks, and there were people round these and the bookstalls. Orange sodium lighting freckled the pavement between shadows of plane trees bordering the road. Some shops re-opened at our approach. Their proprietors were anxious to help, but nobody had a padlock. We were about to abandon our search outside a shop displaying a plastic bowl of water in which a tangle of striped snakes writhed terminally (was *that* what we had for dinner?) when someone said in English:

"Excuse me, do you have a problem? May we help?" We explained about the padlock to the two young men. They looked doubtful, but one thought he knew a place, if we could catch it before it closed. They came from Bejing, we discovered, where they had studied English for two years at college, and kept it up since with a programme on Radio Bejing . . . "but it is wonderful to talk to English people!"

The younger man, with the fine-boned build of the northern Chinese, told me that he made his living as an artist. I was impressed. I had heard that only the specially talented could achieve this in China. I told him that my hobby was watercolour painting. His face lit up.

"My studio is very near. Please come and see my work. It is my home too." Then, seeing our hesitation: "My wife will be there." So we discarded caution and accepted.

We left the wide main street and found ourselves in an unlit alleyway. The ground was rough, and our companions produced torches to guide us. On each side concrete apartment blocks soared, with the sky a jar-edged patch of lighter darkness far above. Curious people looked from lighted doorways at the sound of our voices. We climbed a staircase outside an apartment block, and halted on the tenth floor, a narrow landing, onto which opened several iron doors with reinforced glass panels. Our friend opened the nearest door. We had arrived.

The harsh fluorescent light made us blink. Yuhang's wife, a frail looking girl wearing a floral shirt and black trousers, looked startled. She spoke no English, but shook our hands and smiled shyly. The room was about thirteen feet square. The walls and ceiling were white, the uncovered concrete floor was painted maroon. Opposite, a window stared like an unlidded eye into the night. The window wall was almost entirely occupied by a large double bed with a pink candlewick counterpane. Down the centre of the room was a long table covered with felt, and at one end of this was a collection of paintbrushes and ready-mixed pigments in ceramic jars. Along the wall with the door in it stood an enormous yellow-and-black tartan settee. The fourth wall was filled by a wooden dresser, behind whose sliding glass doors could be seen various personal items – photographs, a spray of plastic flowers and a toy panda. There was just room for a Chinese-sized person to squeeze between the furniture. We sat on the settee. We saw no sign of heating or air conditioning, nor cooking and washing facilities, which we assumed must be communal. Paints on scraps of paper, vibrant with colour and life, brightened the walls.

Yuhang showed us his photograph album.

"Here is my art teacher": short, sturdy, unsmiling, in a Mao suit and rimless spectacles.

"He is a very famous Chinese artist," interjected Zhiqiang. It appeared that Yuhang was considered quite a protégé: several photographs were of him and his mentor beside various paintings.

"Here is our wedding." They were still unsmiling, standing in a formal line before somebody else's dresser. "We have been married for a year now. Maybe in two years . . . maybe three . . ." his voice wished the time away, "we can have our baby." One child. The focus for all the love, unfulfilled hopes, unrealised ambitions; a great burden for small shoulders. The pages turned.

"These are paintings from my first exhibition." Many were traditional, in monochrome, but with his individuality clearly showing. Some were more modern, still very "Chinese".

"These are of Tibet. I went there recently. I am fascinated by the Tibetan women!" One picture caught my attention. A girl's profile, with an enigmatic eye fixed upon some distant point, but among the dark fronds of her hair a miniature cameo of a moonlit ruin like a Greek temple, with people casting long shadows. The base of her neck blended into a landscape.

"Yes, that is different – an experiment, a kind of fantasy." He laughed apologetically. "But I sold it, to a Canadian."

"I should have liked to buy it if you hadn't," I said.

Soon the table was covered with his paintings. We all bought one, at a ridiculously low price for work superior to anything else we had found. However, he was obviously delighted, and on a sudden impulse pressed a 50 yuan note (about £10) into his friend's hand.

Pride was hurt. Anger crackled in the confined space as the older man tried to return the note and, meeting resistance, grabbed hold of Yuhang's shoulders and shook him, speaking vehemently in Chinese. Yuhang's wife, who had been seated on the bed, jumped up in alarm. Afraid that their dispute would become really physical, I caught their arms.

"Please don't fight, it will spoil a wonderful evening!"

"No – don't fight." They backed off, anger simmering.

Later, as we walked back, carrying our paintings wrapped carefully in pages of the *China Daily,* Yuhang explained.

"You see, my friend is a talented photographic designer, but he works for a State Company, for a low wage. I wanted to share my good fortune with him. Friendship is more important than money, would you agree?" I hoped that the anger between them was short-lived, and that he found some more diplomatic way to share his largesse. We stopped a hundred yards from the floodlit tower of our hotel.

"Come inside. We will buy you a drink." They declined reluctantly.

"No, we cannot enter tourist hotels. If we come in with you, very soon someone, maybe a policeman, would come over. He would not be polite." He made his voice rough. "'What is *your* business *here?*' He would take our names and addresses, and we would know that if we did not leave immediately things may be difficult for us in the days ahead." I asked him why. He shrugged.

"I think they believe if we fraternise too much with western people we may want to be like them. We may even try to leave and go to the West." His smile was ironic beneath the street lamp. "Did you not notice? There are not enough people in China!"

As we parted, he handed something to Mary. "You were looking for this, I think." It was a small padlock.

Back in the Jinling we treated ourselves to a nightcap in the Revolving Restaurant. A band played an up-tempo version of *You are my Sunshine* and a few couples bobbed primly on the dance floor. A group of Japanese men pursued the serious business of getting communally drunk. Outside, Nanjing completed a slow revolution, serpents of sodium orange among vertical columns of lighted apartment windows, and above all the random geometry of the stars and a crescent moon. Behind one of those windows an artist may be working. Thank you for our look into your China.

MARK GREEN

ROCK FEVER

The young couple on the beach were having a row of the cold, quiet, intense type. Pale-skinned, freshly sunburned like ourselves, they were recent arrivals. They were on a special holiday, as Bermuda is an expensive place to visit – their honeymoon, perhaps? The thought shocked me. Later, she was staring at the sky with fury in her eyes. He was snorkelling just beyond the surf, kicking his flippers with unnecessary force.

I thought back to our arrival, fresh from the grit of England's second city. A polished holiday, rather than rough-cut travel. Some people cycle across Africa or hike the canyon – things which I would like to do as well, but this was to be luxury in paradise, just right for a recovery from work. Nothing unique to write about, I had thought, imagining the sweaty hiker returning home with the seeds of a massive novel germinating in his head. Or his shoes, maybe. But now, I wasn't sure. I had never seen a society like this, where scenes like the one on the beach seemed so weirdly out of place. Why was it so different?

At the airport, the customs official had all the time in the world.

"Stayin' for long? Three weeks, alrighty." She filled in the form with ponderous care, while we chafed, eager to finish the journey.

"With friends and relatives, eh? Their names? Oh yes, I know Patricia." We looked at each other in surprise. She was obviously not surprised – here, as we soon found out, everyone knows everyone else, and a neighbourly spirit extends over the small, straggling islands. People meet continually by chance, to happily exchange gossip and complaints about their neighbours. Another unwanted pregnancy, the loudness of a party – news called out across the street, or between cars at the traffic lights.

"Yes, knowed her these years gone," she continued. The vagueness, the restful drawl, were a first taste of life here, sunsoaked and slow. Take your time, have a nice stay. We were sure we would.

The taxi driver flashed an easy smile.

"Hello there, what's happening." It was a greeting, not a question.

We slid into the heat of the car. During our short ride, he bipped the horn four times, while the winding lanes revealed that most of the island was a gigantic garden. He was waving recognitition to passing friends; the car horn is not a weapon. Three bips, what's-hap-nin', hey, you take care. He got lost near our journey's end, and strolled out to find the right way. We sat on a wall, already free of the impatience of arrival. Mellow out, they say, and I could feel the customary hurry dissolving, like a sweet stuck in the throat, easing its way down. The pastel walls, white roofs and lush gardens shimmered down to the sky-blue harbour. Mellow out.

As he ambled back he took a few minutes to chat with someone, while we asked a schoolboy for directions; his courtesy was American in style. Yes sir, yes ma'am, my pleasure. And have a nice day, always have a nice day. I had never liked American catchphrases, but now I saw that I had been prejudiced by their worst uses. Or perhaps, as it was a special day, I was seeing the whole place through rose-tinted glasses . . .

I'm not sure when they came off, but I found at some time that I had learned a little about the darker underside of the dazzling views. Under the noon sun the white roofs and yachts flash like diamonds in the far islands. That one there would be St. David's island, low-flying and hazy, looking from where we stood on the main island like a patch of bottle-green paint poured into the sea. A place where tourists and long-term visitors seldom go, where the smiles are still friendly but the manner more aloof. This recess of the island chain is called the most characteristically Bermudian part of the whole, acting as a bastion of their identity in a place whose culture, financial interests and dialogue are almost entirely imported. Perhaps Britain supplies a colonial jackboot along with prosperity, or perhaps the tinges of re-sentment are unjustified – but certainly I occasionally felt a sense of being watched. "Come to the less well-known beaches if you must, but we may stare at you."

Normally they don't, though. The small party of Bermudians is easy to spot among the tourists on the beach. The tourists snorkel and sunbathe, often wearing Walkmans, while the Bermudians have bar-becues and dance to music from large cassette players. Once, when some racist comments were shouted by visitors to their country, they simply ignored it all, their civilised ease based upon observing the line, understated but always present, between themselves and the rest.

A squall blows up with astonishing speed. Remember the ship-wreck scene in *The Tempest,* supposedly set here, the archetypal Bermuda Triangle storm? The Bermudians, by their art, have most cunningly vanished. We, the tourists, tramp off the beach, sandy, bed-raggled and uncomfortable. Some wear pouts: we didn't pay for this. But the storm is a sight well worth seeing – the sea, normally as blue as a baby's eye, is grey and frothing; the palm trees fifty yards away are shadowy, thrashing hands. Twenty minutes later the sun is out on the empty sands, and there is the surprising sense that the shoreline merely coincides with the human pleasure for which it seems designed. Beauty above and below the waves, innocent and then suddenly ferocious.

Some previous dignitary must have liked the connection with *The Tempest:* Ariel Sands and Prospero Lane feature on the map. Allusions to old mother England, as in the place-names Devonshire, Warwick, Somerset and St. George's, are of the quiet everyday type. The more assertive influences of accent, diet and television are American. The English Sports Shop is full of loud check jackets and golfing trousers, while the English colonial spirit sleeps on in an architecture of verandahs, sash windows and high-ceilinged rooms. Driving on the left is the only forceful reminder that this inheritance is still making itself felt.

And you can occasionally still see descendants of the old school hanging on here. I knew the ageing man standing in the surf was one of them – he wore very long Bermuda shorts, a long-sleeved shirt rolled up, glasses, and a military tash. I asked him the time and he seemed mildly surprised to hear my accent.

"Yes, of course I can tell you. It's . . .", old-fashioned watch, "twenty minutes past four." Here American culture has overrun and largely assimilated the British past, but this man, in wisdom or stubbornness, would have none of that. When I looked back he was watching the sea washing his feet, as though trying to remember what had gone missing.

I was amused to see a house called Tally Ho. Chocs Away would surely be next door, I thought; but no, there was just the one. Its inhabitants would be the people I saw later at the airport. A woman was seeing her young son off on the flight to Heathrow, her cut crystal accents showing that he was bound for Eton, Westminster or similar. His distress showed that it was to be his first time away, a new boy in the world of playing fields, prep and Homer. Interestingly, he already had the beginning of a stiff upper lip, though it trembled and failed him when we were asked to board. Soon the islands were a small speckle of light in the dark ocean, and I thought not so much of barracuda, coral, and nights loud with tree-frogs, as of how the boy would slowly learn that home was not down there but in Britain. Few families visit for longer than a decade. "Rock fever" is the name sometimes given to their unrest – the desire for wider landscapes than the pocket-sized beauty of the land allows. Our hosts had given us some insight into this feeling.

"Winter here can be boring, especially on Sundays. Sometimes we drive down to St. George's, where the land ends. Then we drive back." Imagine them standing on the headland, looking out across four thousand miles of Atlantic towards the familiar scenes (and low pay) of home . . . but still, to a tourist, the boy's childhood home seemed a place purpose-built for happiness, and his mood was far more comprehensible than that of the couple on the beach. I wondered, too, if the loss which he felt was a tiny part of the feelings of the British down there – that some time Bermuda would surely be given up by Britain as an unjustifiable possession, a beautiful but outdated gem.

ALTHEA KAYE

FOREST RESTAURANT

I was directed, wordlessly, to the tree-trunk stool. I would have much preferred the long stump that was touched by the rays of the sun filtering thinly through the dense pine forest, but when I am unsure of a situation, especially one in a foreign country, I tend to do as I am told.

Obedience, however, was only part of it. It was now way past tiffin and I was hungry. Pavlovian-like, I knew food was coming. *What* was to be served, though, I didn't know. My breakfast some six hours earlier had consisted of corn soup which had been a euphemism of a cornstarch gruel decorated with a half-dozen yellow kernels; a bowl of rice; a large cube of cold bean curd in soya; and a small wizened piece of fried fish curled elegantly on a fan of pickled radish.

After that eclectic breakfast, I suppose it seemed only natural that I should be lunching, all alone, at a stonewall table with a pool in the middle, in a pine rain forest, far from anywhere. The restaurant – if indeed, it could be called that – was on Shikoku Island, the smallest of the four main islands of the Japanese archipelago.

I had spent the night in Uwajima on the western coast of Shikoku. This morning, on my way to Matsuyama on the northern shore to be initiated into the rituals of a Japanese bath at the famed Dogo spa, I had been quelling my hunger pangs with handfuls of smoked almonds washed down with occasional swigs of mineral water from my battered red canteen.

Then, unexpectedly and suddenly, I came across this restaurant-in-the-glade as I rounded one of the myriad curves of mountainous Shikoku (did you know the land mass of Japan is seventy-five per cent mountains?). A huge vertical sign materialised, offering, in big black flowing characters: Noodles.

The restaurant proper – I never found out its name – was quite un-like any I had ever been in, in Japan or anywhere else. It was completely hidden from the road. To get to it I had to clamber down thirty-two stone steps and cross a carpet of pine needles to a motley conglomeration of open-sided huts. A small red bridge unnecessarily connected two huts. It had been erected for purely aesthetic reasons, since customers could walk around it.

The dining room was, like the other structures, under thatch and was separated from the kitchen by a flimsy bamboo screen. The kitchen, such as it was, was dark, cool and enclosed by equally flimsy woven matting.

A small shrine stood to the left of this *al fresco* dining complex.

As I waited for my meal, I inspected the table – a round stone wall encircling a small pool, home to several dozen tiny goldfish. In the centre of this small lagoon a miniature Japanese garden had been erected. Around the perimeter of this wall an inverted rain gutter was embedded, with icy cold water, diverted from a nearby spring, flowing through. At intervals on the narrow ledge between the duct and the pond were a bottle of soy sauce, a container of the sinus-clearing green horseradish, *wasabi,* a small bowl of chopped scallions, and a sugar dispenser, as well as a bamboo container of chopsticks.

Customers sat on tree stumps. And behind these stools, every now and then, were, inexplicably, empty blue tin pails.

A middle-aged woman in a white smock came and placed a small glass bowl in front of me, along with a steaming rolled washcloth (the custom of all Japanese restaurants). She then proceeded to mix up a sauce of soya, a haphazard dash of sugar, a dollop of *wasabi* and a large spoonful of scallions. She left, I presumed, to return with some food.

As I waited, patiently surveying this whole improbable scene – the pool with the languid goldfish, my bowl of sauce, that special silence of the forest – I suddenly noticed a cluster of cellophane noodles float past me in the flowing spring water. Then another. And another.

My brain clicked. I pulled out a pair of chopsticks and fished out the next mound of noodles as it tried to sail by. Holding it aloft to drain, I dunked the strands into the prepared sauce. The cold noodles, coated in the tarted-up soya, was ambrosial. The waitress beamed at me – the ignorant foreign child had figured out what to do.

"Take as long as you wish, and eat till your tummy is full," she said in Japanese. "And when your sauce gets too diluted, dump it." Ah, the reason for the blue buckets.

I ate with only the gurgling of the water as company. The noodles kept coming, keeping pace with my chewing, and when I was joined by three schoolteachers on holiday (I wondered if they had come across this by accident, too, or whether they had knowingly planned an excursion through the sparsely-inhabited mountains), the white translucent mounds came meandering by at shorter intervals.

How did the noodles know? A woman sat in the kitchen behind the bamboo screen and dropped handfuls into this unusual dumb waiter.

If you want to know the location of this restaurant, all I can give you is the entry in my journal: "On a curve on Route 378 which hugs the northwestern coastline of Shikoku and about six or seven miles west of Nagahama."

You can't miss it. But carry some almonds, just in case.

BOB TURVEY

EVERYMAN'S FINLAND

My wife goes to Finland each summer because she's a Finn. She takes Sam who is nine and a naturalist, and William who's six . . . well, just William. I go when we can afford it.

The plan this year is to go by ferry and car. Being a prudent soul I check out the insurance small print. We have eight hours to drive across Sweden to catch the next ferry. We've done it before, and it takes six. So what if we break down for three hours and miss the connection?

"We don't pay," says the AA lady. "You have to be mechanically incapacitated for twelve hours."

We decide to do without, save the £100 and trust to the potential goodwill of the ferry company. We toss across the North Sea, and the naturalist checks out the inside of the sea-sickness bags.

Sunday seems to be a go-slow at Gothenburg docks. We took the precaution of arriving early at Harwich, so we could get off first at Gothenburg. We are actually the next to the last car to come off the boat. We spend forty-two minutes on the quayside before we hit the road.

Six hours later, at 8.03pm, we pull into Stockholm's Värtahamnen harbour. Quite remarkable, that even though the tickets cost so much the company doesn't print the name of the harbour on the ticket. There are, of course, *two* harbours from which you can sail to Finland. We know where to go only because we've done it before.

The second we hit the quayside we know there's trouble – *no queue of cars*. We flourish our tickets.

"I'm sorry," says the little girl, "the *Wellamo's* run aground. If you hurry you might just squeeze on that boat over there."

That boat is going to Helsinki, not Turku, *and* we wouldn't have a cabin. The exercise turns out to be academic anyway, because as we roar towards it the stern gate shuts. We go into the terminal because William has diarrhoea.

When he's finished we plough into the milling throng. A ferry will typically take two thousand people. You can picture the scene. Babel.

The *Silja Line* girls are very pretty, but totally unhelpful.

"We warned everyone on the Swedish radio not to come."

I let my wife scream and shout. She gets nowhere.

I pass the time of day with a morose Norwegian leaning against a pillar. He was actually on the *Wellamo*.

"There we were, on this brand-new computer-controlled floating miracle, threading our way through the islands. Suddenly the lights all go out. The generator is gone. No back up. So the computer – *phut!* No navigation. Fifteen minutes later we slide onto a rocky island. Everyone rushes to the bow, leans over. Small house on the top of the hill. Light comes on, then a torch starts to walk down towards us. Torch stops, points upwards, runs the boat.

"*Mmm, Wellamo,* says a voice. Torch then inspects where the boat has run aground. *Well, that's not done my potatoes much good.*"

Nice story. I'm sure it's apocryphal. Guy has bigger problems than I have – his car is still on the *Wellamo,* now back in Finland; his cat, parrot and mother-in-law are stuck in the terminal. And his wife is expecting them home for dinner in Oslo. He looks philosophical.

Round about this time I wonder if I made the right decision about insurance. It seems I did – for other people are reading the small print in their policies and finding all sorts of things. Like maybe you can claim – but you don't get the money until you get back to the UK. And like you can only claim for a hotel if the delay until you get on the next *scheduled* ferry is more than twelve hours – and the next ferry leaves in eleven.

My turn to berate the officials comes round. We've just been told that the Company's responsibilities under Swedish Maritime law *(bilingual copy available for inspection at the Company's Head Office)* are nil, and official policy can be summed up in one word. *Tough.*

I put myself in the guy's position. His problem of course is that there are no places on the next boat.

"All you want to do is get rid of me, and all I want is a place on the boat."

He nods.

"You overbook me on the next boat and I'll go away."

I know it's done regularly on aircraft, and invariably there are enough cancellations so you get on. Can you do it on boats, though?

He looks at me, then nods, makes the arrangements and I go away.

We are allowed to sleep in the unfinished terminal. Even though we've got sleeping bags and rugs the beautiful marble floor sucks body heat. In the morning we get a free coffee. Wow.

We breeze onto the boat. Overbooking works.

My wife tells me the trip through the Åland archipelago is a most beautiful journey, slipping slowly through islands, skirting skerries, passing rocks. I wouldn't know. I was asleep.

We finally roll out of Turku harbour. William has fallen asleep. Hours later he wakes up, and looks around.

"Where are we Daddy?"

"Finland."

"Where are all the people?"

His question set the tone of the holiday. We start to slow down, to wind down. We drive deeper and deeper into the forest. We come to the ferry to Grandad's island. Finland has ferries like Britain has bridges. They're free. They chug up to the landing stage, the end gate crashes down with a thud. Big lugs on it lock into the road surface. Cars drive off. We drive on. The gate crashes up, the ferry throbs across the strait. The gate crashes down again. We drive off.

Finally we arrive at the house. Grandad and Grandma are there. Uncle is very happy to see us. Too happy, actually. Good job we've hidden the duty free. The boys roll off to see the farm animals.

Finland is enjoying one of the best summers in living memory. Blue skies every day. Almost too hot. We swim in the lake every day. Watch gulls mob a buzzard. Row over to the little island to look for sundew plants. The only sound is of insects, of lapping water, of the lads splashing and the grebes barking across the lake.

Going to the outhouse causes a living confetti of butterflies to rise up from the flowers – small blues and coppers. Camberwell Beauties are ten-a-penny here.

"Why are there so many butterflies?" I ask the naturalist.

He screws his nose. "They like it here," he says.

The right answer from a child.

Finland is fish. Sobered up, Uncle goes out nightly and trawls the lake. Every visitor to Finland encounters the ubiquitous, small and silvery *muikku*. It took me years to find its English name. And it doesn't mean a thing to most English people – *the vendace*. But freshly caught, smoked so that its skin turns orange-brown and translucent as chocolate wrappers – then it really translates as a gourmet's delight, eaten skin, bones and all. The lads help Uncle smoke them. That's half the fun, getting smoked yourself.

In summer Finland is full of old aunts who inhabit little cottages by the lakeside. They have gas fridges, cold beer and snappy dogs. They are great if they are *your* aunties. Fortunately several are, so we endure the dogs and days on end are spent lying on floating jetties, rocking gently and looking up at the sky. Do you know, if you watch small clouds on sunny days they often evaporate and disappear completely?

We go from island to island in boats. Fences are rare in Finland, and usually put up only to stop moose blundering onto the road. William can't quite shake off his British sense of property and trespassing.

"Who owns this island? Don't they mind us being here? Why can we just come here and behave like it's ours?"

Eventually one of the old ladies explains the matter at William's level.

"Every man owns the right to walk in the forest, and as long as you don't damage it or the land, you can go where you like."

William is satisfied.

We go home eventually via North Germany, and spend the insurance money on wine. Most attractive policy I've ever seen!

And as we're putting the kettle on, and opening all the mail, we notice William writing. It's a card to Mr Everyman, to say thank you.

VALERIE TUFNELL

LAZY DAYS ON DAL

The little man appeared soundlessly on the verandah, holding aloft a shiny grey suit to which he urged us to attend. "I am tailor," he announced. "Savile Row not better." He was also, it emerged, in common with most Kashmiris, a politician, with a zeal for independence tempered only by admiration for General Zia. To India he made distant reference, contemptuous of its democracy, but reserving a particular scorn for the Hindu tailors. "Father army tailor," he exclaimed with pride – which confidence provoked a responsive bellow from within the houseboat: "Derzi wallah! He was a derzi wallah!"

There followed a long, only partly comprehensible exchange, in which derzi, dhobi, and sundry other wallahs featured, culminating in extraction of dog-eared photograph from battered wallet – Bill, ex-army, India, '44, in front of a curiously deserted Taj Mahal. "The hat, Guy Perron's hat, was all wrong, we never wore them at that sissy tilt with the brim up."

Cloth samples having been duly fingered and admired, 'Tasty Tailors of Kashmir', with the inevitable promise to return later, stepped neatly into his shikara and paddled away across the lake. We retired within to the chintzy splendour of the *Khyber Palace* for tea, dry yellow madeira cake and contemplation of the visitors' book – the previous occupants had obviously succumbed to the exhortations of laundry man and tailor – both had "a good mention".

The boat, "five-star de luxe with three stars", followed the standard Victorian design, a long bone-coloured cedarwood structure with a landing ghat for the shikaras. The verandah, with its massive pillared canopy resembling an old four-poster, gave way to an imposing drawing room, decked out with standard lamp and tapestried chaise longue with "matching" chairs piled high with crewelled cushions. A cabinet with cabriole legs, filled with empty liquor bottles, proudly displayed by Mr Loan, the Muslim house boy, cheap bright prints and a "welcome" wall-hanging fashioned from pink felted paper and varnished shells, the whole illuminated by an enormous glass chandelier.

At least, in theory. At dusk when the verandah lights and the over-large television sets were switched on, the strain often proved too much for the system. Paddling back across the lake we could barely discern the boats, eerily lit by candle glimmer, while even Srinagar lay plunged in gloom behind us.

To conserve energy we would sit, savouring the resinous smell of cedar, watching television in the half-light. Rajiv Gandhi seemed curiously amateurish and waxen, resembling the matinée idol billboards of the local cinema, or the advertising hoardings in the new town.

Life on the lake is oddly self-contained. Only from the roof of the boat can there be appreciation of a land-bound existence; from this vantage, surprisingly impressive half-timbered houses can be seen, populated by large and busy families with well-fed animals. From here too it seemed possible to walk on water to the lake's edge, supported by the densely woven mesh of lotus leaves which choke the narrow channels between the boats.

The houseboats are at the mercy of hawkers and travellers of every persuasion, but few are without interest, and the stuff of existence, luxury and necessity, can be bartered, haggled and traded from the comfort of the verandah.

Primitive shikaras carried pink-tinged ivory, weighty jewellery from Ladakh, *papier mâché,* crewell embroidery, Kashmiri cloth, and always the battered tin box with special treasures inside. The wrinkled Tibetan features of the laundry man appeared above a pile of much-boiled shirts and trousers, pressed and creased to razor precision; saffron pedlars offered a few strands for thirty rupees, inveighing against cheap and harmful imitations. There were tea boats, boats bearing spices and powdered dyes, vegetable boats, and grocery boats laden with Limca, Efco apple juice and Torino, watery orange optimistically labelled "keep cool"; ancient Cadbury's chocolate tins containing equally aged grey milk chocolate, rendered too powdery to melt, and the rough grey, aptly named 'Scruples' toilet paper, bearing the legend "quality in motion", an irony much marked on our boat.

In the early morning, as the houseboys unwound themselves from blankets on the verandahs, came the flower boats, blazingly decked with dahlias, marigolds and gladioli. A sale was agreed: two grubby white envelopes of identical seeds, one of which promised white lilies, the other, less believably, pink. Then there was the tailor, reinforced now by his sprightly, wizened little father, sitting cross-legged on the dining room floor.

The splendidly tinselled shikaras with their heart-shaped paddles

Houseboats and shikaras on Lake Dal, Kashmir. (*Lazy Days on Dal*)

The largest reclining Buddha in the East. *(Where the Lion Never Sleeps)*

Time for a quick cuppa in Singapore's Serangoon Road, or in the garden of the famous Raffles Hotel. *(Where the Lion Never Sleeps)*

offered an escape of sorts. *Vale of Kashmir* and *Sephesalar* were ours to command, and we were conveyed like bloated pashas around the weed-infested by-ways behind the houseboats, where Kashmiris tend floating vegetable gardens and make a living fashioning crafts for the Government Emporium.

The open lake was more hazardous. The ubiquitous pedlars were reinforced by raiding parties of engaging, slippery children, who tossed freshly-picked lotus blooms on board and cried for satisfaction in baksheesh.

But these are swiftly outdistanced, and away from the houseboats towards the Causeway and the Moghul gardens is serenity: time to observe the deft accuracy of the kingfishers, watch the outline of the Pir Panjal mountains, and ponder the possibility of tea on the spreading green lawns of the Oberoi Palace Hotel.

Apart from the odd tourist shikara, the leisurely traffic here comprises weed barges piled dangerously high with vegetation trawled from the lake. These floating islands are expertly manipulated by diminutive women pilots who will use their catch for cattle feed and fertiliser. More dramatic is the visitation of the great blue-green dredger which rumbles uncomfortably close to the houseboats, clawing the weed from the lake bed and masticating it noisily in its metal insides.

Towards Dal gate and the old town, the lake is more densely populated. The houseboats give way to the primitive single-room doonga boats, grey-bleached barges with rudimentary slatted wooden roofs, inhabited all year round. In sombre contrast to the cosmetic gaiety of the *New Neil Armstrong*, *The Balmoral* and *The Khyber*, these serve as both home and business, and the variety of goods and services provided mirrors the activity on the Boulevard.

The Boulevard runs along the south side of the lake and is the main artery into the town of Srinagar. As such it teems with prosperous Kashmiri life, on foot, on bicycle or Vespa, in auto-rickshaws emitting noxious fumes, or Ambassador taxis, caught in a Morris Oxford time warp, circa 1954.

At the end of the Boulevard is Jan's Bakery, discovered to be the best and most hygienic of the cake shops, with an ingenious fly-catching machine comprised of whirring mesh rollers under ultra-violet lights. Here, alongside the inevitable dry madeira, were splendid cream confections, satisfying crunchy nut and fig cake, chocolate cookies and an extraordinary fantasy of a wedding cake, rising upwards in biliously coloured tiers.

A selection of the more durable cakes augmented the rather odd blend of English and Indian cuisine, produced in murky quarters at the back of the boat by a villainous looking cook. Chapatis, omelette and dal were a favourite, followed by banana fritters or doughnuts. But if the food was odd, the conversation was stranger still. We talked of India and army days, of chokidars and furloughs, of havildars and subadars, until softly, through the shadows we heard, "Very fine cloth, Sahib, Savile Row not better!"

WHERE THE LION NEVER SLEEPS

Lion City, S.E.A. I am awoken by the boom of tropical rain. Fat warm drops fly through the twisted wrought-iron shutters, landing with a hiss on heated flesh. Tess is humped on a nearby bunk, reluctant to face the fearful day. A strong odour of sour milk and durians drifts from the communal kitchen, mingling with the sluggish air circling the Bencoolen St Buildings. In the gloom of the graffiti-ed corridor, the catlike owner eyes me with suspicion. No, we are not pinching the other guests' food, and yes, we probably will stay one more night. In this seedy concrete dive? No choice – jet-lag ensured we missed today's train. The dragons are already breathing fire down our aching necks. Welcome to the Orient, stay awhile, let us show you our island of delights.

He awakes stiff with dirt and exhaustion, cotton khaki soaked in sweat. The smell of blood and smoke and urine has forced itself through the already unbearable pall of heat up to the seventh floor, where he is stationed to spot enemy flashes. Families of Indians and Chinese sleep huddled on stairways which wind down the building; their babies don't whimper, because this is war. Civilians and soldiers, wounded or stranded with nothing to say. He remembers the terrible silence which hangs over them, as heavy as the blanket of smoke from cheap cigarettes, and the seeping fumes of Australian wine.

First stop, the umbrella shop. Five Singapore dollars for a flimsy parasol which whisks inside out as soon as we step into the thundering melee. Flooded storm drains line the streets; it is whispered snakes swim in their murky depths. We splash and stumble whilst Lion City dwellers pass smartly with quick, accomplished steps. Chinese, Malays, Indians, Tamils, it is the Singapore lunch hour; we are in the way.

A man cycles by, bent double, his dog standing proudly on a box on the back. In the Telok Ayer Food Emporium, young bloods lounge and stare. I wish Tess hadn't worn her shorts, even though they are sturdy army issue, set off to perfection by her baseball boots. Ravenous, we devour sweet and sour pork, tofu, bean shoots and rice, and lurch, recovered, into the stormy, perspiring streets.

Was it forty-five years ago you were here, my own flesh and blood, my father? Twenty years old and – we have laughed at the irony – defending Singapore! Can someone please tell me what I'm doing on this self-imposed pleasure cruise, with no thoughts on my mind beyond coconut jelly and mango ice-cream? Do we tramp the same land on such different grounds?

Escaping the wide, white boulevards of Bras Basah and Serangoon Road, we cross the river to Chinatown. The churning brown waters rock with bumboats and loaded sampans. The streets are cluttered. Bougainvillea spills over cracked neon script, Chinese lanterns hang in doorways, pale green follies front cheap hotels. We drink rice wine issued from an ancient silver urn, while the din of a ghetto-blaster pelts the steamy air. A roadside calligrapher carefully paints gold letters of immaculate intricacy onto red cloth, and a duck vendor calls his wares as we pass. "Waxed dusk and sausages, waxed dusk and baby meats . . ."

December 1941, news arrives. Orders are to march up to Kota Bahru on the Malay/Thai border and halt the invasion. Some hope! On a belly full of rice, with VD, the runs, and driven half-mad by prickly heat? OK, chaps, best foot forward, this is the challenge you've been waiting for.

From the Hindu Temple in Tank Road, a six-headed god glowers between high-rise flats. We press past *McDonalds*-chomping crowds at The People's Market and emerge, with a gasp, into the cool, bare arms of Central Park. Lovers as clean and creamy as lotus blossoms glide giggling down palm-lined lanes.

Official Singapore squeaks cleanly as it moves along finely-honed government grooves, newly brushed and washed, severe and bland. Don't throw chewing gum on the pavement; don't spit, toss litter, or, men, grow long hair. This is Lion City, an animal taunted by a giant mask, dancing in time to crashing gongs. A city where mutinous outdoor barbers snip their customers' heads, oblivious to the piles of black hair mingling with melon rinds in the bluff, colonial road.

His first night in the jungle. Dad stands watch through the lonely night. In the early hours it pours with rain. He rips off his uniform, tears off his topee and stands naked, off guard, the fresh rain thrashing his angry red skin.

I purchase a small tin of lotion for "frecles, boils and smoothness of skin". We visit the Temple of One Thousand Lights, where Tess buys tiger balm, drains a glass of papaya and looks pleased with herself. Still haunted by the invisible dragon's breath, I follow meekly in her wake, hopping over storm drains like an anxious goat.

The day steams and lengthens. We barter thickly for jackfruit and fat, sweet bananas, return to our fan-blown beshuttered room and sleep. At dusk we are disturbed by the presence of the cat-eyed owner in our room. His feline gaze slides over our bodies, recoiling under gauze-thin sheets, towards the shrivelled fruit skins, maps and water pills hurled around the place. Accusing us of leaving the fan on too long, he demands instant dollars for another night. Oh, another whole night in shanty town. We pay to get rid of him, and share a ripe mangosteen – it is like hairy testicles on the outside, red and angry, and so rich and sweet within. We collect our thoughts and our pursebelts, and soldier on into the hot, dark, dirty streets.

His best mate was killed in Kota Bahru. The night watches came to an end. Driven down country, they slept rough under the warm stars and, two months later, re-crossed the Johor Baharu border back into Singapore.

Night time in Bugis Street, ex-haunt of transvestites, swept away like the debris that will never disappear. Stalls line the road. A bright white hissing gas lamp illuminates propped-up cardboard photos of human torsos, horribly scarred, acupuncture needles hanging from their flesh. Further on, a prostrate man lies blindfold, encircled by the crowd. Brandishing a rusty dagger, his healer/magician spits a hoarse stream of invocation into a microphone, so that his very throat seems to disgorge into the metal and crack over our bare heads. A fat white Navy officer bumps sheepishly by on a trishaw, a woman in a skin-tight sarong perched unsmiling at his side. Scattering lychee shells with his wheels, the Malay driver looks neither to left nor right.

We are spilled helplessly into the night market. Lurid Indian sweet-meats glare alongside banana leaf packets of saffron rice, while sticks of satay char on methylated spirit coals.

The soldiers burn their own weapons, and open bottles of whisky, wine and gin to pour down the drains. The roads are awash with blood and liquor, shell-shocked friends and Red Cross vans. And the only thing left to do is wait.

We are feeling wicked. Our plans increase. The Raffles Hotel – to be taken by storm! Tess, let us lounge in wicker discomfort in Somerset Maugham's bar, let us hear tinkled laughter 'twixt the chink of our eighth frosted sling. Surreal oversized raffles palms flap like unbalanced giants in the artificial breeze. It's too, too much. Releasing ourselves from the ex-pat poet's prattle, we breathe in the fumes of hot, tropical traffic and non air-con air.

15th February, 1942. Singapore falls. The Cathay building is evacuated and taken over by enemy HQ. Dad is sent on a working party to Changi barracks and celebrates his twenty-first birthday walking seventeen miles to help load booty onto boats bound for Japan.

The blazing figure of Merlion, half lion, half fish, beckons in brilliance from the river's mouth. I run to the quay. Buildings rise like dominoes all around, glittering ominously, clustered together, hiding the past. I feel afraid. The wide, sharp, hot night reveals nothing, conceals everything. I search in vain to make out just one name – the Cathay building, once the tallest in all Singapore. But the sky is like ink. I turn to leave, oppressed by the scented breath of orchid blooms lolling in Memorial Park Land.

Memorial? For all his mates who died as POWs in the camps up north, perhaps? For eating nothing but rice for four years? For amputating gangrenous toes, stealing quinine, building railways in swamps, being beaten alive? Yes, a memorial to those who died. And I a memorial to he who survived.

We return to Bencoolen Street. The hotel is full of mad men, lying drunk and sweating on bunks, laughing, half-naked, and tanned deep brown, their doors flung wide for all to see. Tess and I move through them to our sleazy private suite, justified in our self-imposed and haughty isolation. The battle is over. Outside, the Lion City roars.

MARK SWALLOW

COCO LOCO

The best road sign we ever saw pointed us towards "The Best Most Beautiful Beach In The World", where we lay through the whole hot day.

The beach bar was run by a family with a passion for cocktail experiment. They sent a younger son over to our hammock where he whipped out his machete and decapitated a nearby coconut. Smiling broadly, he poured spirits in from all directions and handed us what they call a Coco Loco.

So we lay, sucking at the strong syrup. We could not argue with the sign. Whoever argued on the Caribbean coast of Mexico?

In the morning we had been the first car down a new road being built, as we drove, by the men of the village and their sons, hurling away rocks and stones before the steamroller. Then we came, greeted by smiles of approval because we seemed so eager to try out the new road.

Contrast that scene with the panicked traffic of Mexico City. Swinging out of an airport car park and into a new country's traffic, its bloodstream, is the strangest feeling. But in Mexico D.F. we feel it more because the blood flows so thick and fast, the city groaning with car sickness. In ten years they say babies will be born with fume-induced brain damage.

Take another look, from the air: Houston, Texas, is punched through with clear blue holes – a city of private swimming pools – but coming into the next stop there is no blue, just grey hardness. We have arrived in Mexico.

That first morning we went to the World Cup press building, the first temple of our journey, a temple of tinted glass and metal, dedicated to football fever. The press corps has been gone a fortnight but video screens continue to flash highlights, keeping the circus going. The wide-faced senorita still serves free drinks and the cleaners brush on.

"Is it all over already?" they ask, and the cohort of electric type-writers buzzes back, "Yes, what are you going to do with us now?"

An English friend is fearing for the country's future: "They have had the circus without the bread," she says. The chief of police, like some Roman emperor, has closed the city's orbital road for the day so that his children can have a motorcycle race. Metro tickets cost more to print than to buy, and the public phones are free because the coin that fits them is now worthless.

At traffic lights on the way to the airport to catch a plane across the Gulf there was some big city charm: a mime artist had found an audience and in white face with painted hands he pulled a lady's car towards him on an imaginary rope. She eased off the brake, rolled forward and smiled through the windscreen; when the lights changed she ladled some coins into his hand as he darted back to the pavement.

We had flown to Merida, capital of the Yucatan region, and bartered enthusiastically for the hire of a small car from agents who posed as rivals. They burst out laughing when we made our decision, for they were all from the same company and great friends.

We took a bus then from a bright blue terminal as fussy as a Victorian palace. Inside the building was a queue in which we stood missing four consecutive departures and watching a boy selling purple foam iguanas. Everyone wanted these whippy reptiles which twitched on the end of a wire, and soon they were scuttling all over the hall.

Drives through the Yucatan are like flat minefields – desolate green scrub for miles around and then a crack and a shudder as our front axle hits a *topos,* speed ramp, which has lain in wait unannounced. Men stride through the villages with T-shirts hitched up over their pot bellies to keep cool – both from the sun and the platefuls of chillis on every bar table.

Back in Merida we pressed our faces against the station fence and eyed Nationales de Mexico, a khaki train of Pullman carriages which would take us west to Palenque. We bought first-class tickets, preparing for an evening of faded splendour and dusty comfort in a thirties cabin. We sat for three hours before even pulling out, and during that time we understood it was going to be an experience of a different kind.

Through the infernal night only the lights from stations cast their glare over the crush within. At 5am a large mother boarded with her two doe-eyed daughters whom she fed with bread, honey and yoghurt. The girls took it politely but screwed up their faces at the yoghurt and exchanged anguished glances while the mother's back was turned to praise her neighbour's turkey.

Was it turkeys in first class, chickens in *segunda?*

Then mother saw us struggling to collect coins for a beer and forced *pesos* upon us. The beer was cool and golden and made us light-headed as the sun rose and the breakfast ritual began in full. At every station a line of children would board and slalom down the aisle with fruit, milk and vegetables, advertised in a well-rehearsed patter. Granny followed with a bucket of *tortillas* arranged in hot petal formation and smelling dully in her wake.

But the line swarmed so fast it was unstoppable. The only transaction we saw was through the window: a woman passed money to the drink boy, the train roaring and jerking forward before he could give her the bottle. He gave gallant chase but realised as he failed that it was his gain and collapsed in triumphant laughter with his friends.

We wandered around Palenque, dazed like so many of the sacrificial victims led there 1,300 years ago. More beautifully sited than any other Indian temple we saw, Palenque glared out from a man-made perch in a jungly hill over Chiapas. The jungle backing with its waterfalls meant the site was not tamed like Chichen Itza, Uxmal, Tulum or even Monte Alban, an earlier Olmec stronghold made by cutting off the top of a mountain.

Such enormous ruins littered our Mexican journey, as did the small towns which rose out of the distance of the Yucatan. They always had arches around the *zocalo,* an esplanade centred on a complacent looking Juarez in bronze. He was the Indians' own hero in the Civil War, assaulting the power of the church in 1860 and now staring across *zocalos* at churches all over the Yucatan.

With one or two definitely urban streets, such places had a certain municipal feel about them; but they were really remote outposts with pigs wallowing in main-road waterholes. We would pull over rather than attempt a meeting with the weekly Coca Cola lorry.

As peculiar as the stylish press agency amidst the squalor of D.F. were the whizzbang thirties buildings dotted around these Yucatan townships. Most housed dentists, but the best example was a streamlined purple cinema in Merida which vied with the cathedral for mass attention on a Saturday night. Beggars were divided as to which they felt it better to parade.

We stand up to greet the machete boy who is back from the bar of The Most Beautiful Beach In The World. He finds another coconut and we reel a little before sitting back in the hammock – the other way round so that we can enjoy a new perspective.

We have been on the trail first plodded by Mayan Indians in the immediate centuries after Christ, and later by the hippies. It is a route dotted with pyramids and beachside cafés all decorated with fantastic images of power and death. The Mayans were largely ignored by the Spanish under Cortes. He made straight for Montezuma's Aztecs and never came back to our area of dense low jungle and beaches, turning gold as they round the Gulf of Mexico and down the Caribbean coast to Belize.

"Such Is Life" said the sign in Las Brisas, an open-air bar where we had two nights of backgammon and a third spent talking to a gentleman just down from D.F. in his 1952 Cadillac with a caravan and plans to set up a rest house and die here in Playa del Carmen. He took us round the back to admire that great mothership, but it was dark so we just felt its huge growth of a chrome bumper up front.

In a hut on the Island of Women off that coast we tried out our new hammock and, swaying there, struck up a friendship with pretty Mexican children next door – all except the young brother who screamed if he saw us. One morning the hammock was gone. The children just smiled and said *la bruja,* the witch, has taken it in the night.

A fiesta cheered us a little, the rhythm pumping out on the *zocalo* full in the face of Juarez. Our eyes fell on one couple among the fifty on the dusty dance floor: a woman with a red-lipped mouth full of gold teeth was swaying her hips for her husband whose T-shirt was hitched up on a pot-belly bared to the evening sun. He too moved with great skill, clucking his head like a cock, almost break-dancing to the blaring sound. They were entrancing to watch and as she led him off she caught our stare and flashed a gold smile.

JULIA TAYLOR

ANYTHING BUT NOODLES

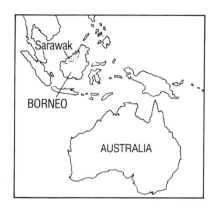

Kuching? Has anyone ever heard of Kuching? Isn't it supposed to be some ancient little wooden harbour town? I wasn't exactly expecting its motorways and fast food outlets, but I'm glad of the hamburgers because the rest of the food in this remote land must be the worst in the world. Even their fried noodles, that South East Asian staple, are a disgrace to the Orient. One decent Chinese restaurant, and that closes for the whole of Chinese New Year – which covers the best part of a week and happens, of course, to be just the time we're in Kuching. Not that I'm in Sarawak for a gourmet fortnight or anything, and goodness knows, after all my years on the road eating whatever's been available, my palate is not the most finely-tuned. But even I can't face those greasy noodles again, and my companion, who used to run his own French restaurant . . . well, I think he'll probably bear the scars of our many dining catastrophes for the rest of his life.

There being no railways and precious few roads, all our travelling is done by boat and plane. We plan to be rowed gently up "the Mighty Rejang River", as the brochures persistently call it, through the tropical rainforest. Instead we are loaded, by means of a single slender plank which causes much wavering of feet and brain, onto one of the fastest commercial boats in the world – a Lamborghini of the boat kingdom whose engines scream as it ferries us out of Kuching Harbour into the open sea, and across the bay to plunge into the mouth of the Mighty Rejang. And mighty it is indeed. It looks about ten miles wide, but we can just make out the tropical rainforest on either bank, overhanging nicely in the style we were promised. Logging stations like the sides of the river, and huge amounts of timber float around waiting for a barge to stop and pick them up. The seven o'clock start proves too much for us and we pass out on deck – an enormous error of judgement as the equatorial sun gets into top gear, aided and abetted by the wind which keeps us just cool enough to ensure that we don't wake up until the faces, necks and chests have been seared off us.

Now Sibu and Kapit look a bit more like your primitive jungle towns, or do they? Old Dayak grannies, members of the biggest tribe in Sarawak, hobble about chewing betel. It's only a couple of decades ago that head-hunting was stopped by the British. Now, instead of a brace of skulls in their shopping bags, it's another form of entertainment – like as not a copy of "Son of Rocky 44" from the Kapit video parlour. The video industry must have done more than any other to shrink the world. Rambo and Rocky have followed me around at least fifteen countries in the past year. The Dayak men have dark blue shapes tattooed on their necks and, so the Kuching Museum has informed us, less public parts of their anatomy pierced with a metal pin. This we cannot attest to.

Food and accommodation continue to worsen, just when we thought they could sink no lower. A Chinese hotel turns out to be a cross betwen a brothel and a pool for unemployed building labourers, with overnight lodging for travellers coming a very poor third. Evil-looking men hang around on every landing, and all the plumbing is unpleasantly blocked. I draw the manager's attention to this. "That's right," he says agreeably, and goes back to fiddling with his Japanese motorbike in the lobby. That night, as I doze uneasily, my companion leaps up from the bed and hurls our rat-infested wastepaper basket out of the fourth-floor window. I don't mind quiet rats, like the one in my room in Thailand who, over the course of seven weeks, ate my entire bar of soap little by little and never once woke me up. But these noisy wastepaper-basket operators are too much to be ignored, even in a semi-conscious state.

My birthday coincides with the first day of the Chinese New Year, which seems pretty auspicious to me. I wake up with the distinct feeling that no white woman has ever spent a birthday in such an obscure corner of the earth. From the oil town of Miri, on the coast near the border with the tiny Sultanate of Brunei, the shared taxi is taking us along dirt roads to the jungle village of Batu Niah in the company of the world's oldest woman, a centuries-old Chinese granny who, it seems, is going to visit her children on their farm for the holiday with enough packages for a prolonged stay. Upon arrival at the homestead, it becomes clear while her provisions are being unloaded that all is not as it should be. She jabbers at me excitedly in Chinese and I eventually see the cause of her distress. The taxi driver has failed to realise that the round box, two feet in diameter, contains a massive cream-and-sugar edifice, hung about with lacy icing in pastel shades. Due to his careless packing, my backpack has fallen on it and he is frantically trying to slide the top layer back into place with one hand and restore the butter cream, which is now smeared around my luggage, with the other. Will the world's oldest woman survive the shock of this indignity? My companion warns me with his customary vicious ankle-kick that I'd better stifle the laughter that's rising in my throat.

For the rest of my birthday, we turn our attention to finding plentiful supplies of Anchor beer and some alternative to fried noodles.

The trees in a tropical rainforest never shed their leaves and do not keep pace with normal seasons. They flower as and when they individually choose, according to some primeval clock deep inside them – another interesting fact for my collection. This is not somewhere I care to walk alone. One step off the path into the dense shiny green vegetation and I'd never be seen again. Maybe I'd become a jungle person and have to eat berries and hunt small tropical rodents. I don't really like to consider the possibility. The ancient trees crackle and sing to each other, and insects and frogs whoop and whirr. These huge flying beetle things, the size of airborne hamsters, and dragonflies as big as blackbirds, were divebombing us last night as we sat under the light reading about the coves we're going to visit. A new stealthy noise sends my brain running into one of its far-flung store-cupboards, trying to remember whether there were or still are tigers in Borneo.

By the the time we reach the caves I'm running with sweat, but this is nothing compared to what the interior of the caves does to me. No part of me remains dry. It's like sightseeing in a Turkish bath with the proportions of St. Paul's Cathedral: a series of dark, dank, vaulted limestone caverns, the largest maybe 200 feet in height. The torch held by our tiny, wiry, wily old local guide, Omar, barely cuts a narrow lighted path through the choking, slippery, dripping gloom as we visit the two industries conducted in that Hell's Kitchen.

A steady stream of men carry out huge baskets of guano produced by the hundreds of thousands of bats and swiftlets that inhabit the caves and fill them with their rustling and twittering. More bizarre yet is the collection, from the roof of the caves, of the little swiftlet nests used for making the now famous birds' nest soup. Yes, really. The men climb up incredibly fragile-looking poles, swaying up to the cave roof where a flimsy workman's gallery has been built. They work in the pitch dark with miners' lamps on their heads putting the nests – miniscule and messy, being composed mainly of swiftlet saliva – into baskets on their backs. This has to be about the most foolhardy job there is. They give us a nestlet as a souvenir, but omit to tell us the recipe so unfortunately I can't try it for supper.

Emerging once more into steamy emerald daylight, I provide an entertaining contrast with Omar. I look as if I've spent the time in a sauna while he looks as refreshed as if he's just had tea on an English summer lawn. But my trials by water aren't over yet. As I dither in my attempt to step onto the perilously rocking boat which is to ferry us across the river, the mud bank gives way and I'm suddenly up to my neck in silty water. When I try to move, this first cousin to the Mighty Rejang swallows me whole. I don't know what to be frightened of first: drowning, or alligators. Together they manage to pump up enough

adrenalin to get me out. Scant sympathy awaits me in the jumpy boat.
I am adjudged to have planned the whole incident with malice
aforethought deliberately to annoy others and call attention to myself.
We take time out for an obligatory sulk, and by the time I'm dry and
smoothed down we are ready to join forces again for another round of
the East-West match, an enduring favourite. Will the two effete Westerners manage to outwit the Chinese brothel-keeper and the ex-head-
hunters, and find something other than greasy fried noodles to eat
tonight?

PETER MAY

THE FLOWERS OF RUWENZORI

You don't need ropes to ascend Mount Ruwenzori – at least, not to get to Hut Kiondo at 4,200 metres. What you do need is stamina.

I saw clouds swirling up the valleys, and hiding the lower peaks as in the distance the hut which was my destination seemed as far away as ever. The air was thin, and the sun merciless. Behind the hut the glacier sparkled and dazzled. I forced my body up the slope: I *must* reach the top of the ridge before the clouds.

Over another hill, then there was the hut. It is on the top of a fifty-foot mound at the end of a razor-edged ridge. I was delighted to see that it was surrounded by dozens of pink and white flowers on the otherwise barren ground.

I am not a climber, barely a walker. This basic tour of Zaire included a four-day walk up Mount Ruwenzori. We were warned that it was usually hidden by clouds, and that the intensity of the rain during the day was exceeded only by the cold at night. At the foot of the mountain the hot humidity made the bundles of banknotes stick together as we counted them out to pay for our ascent. This much for the park fees, so much for camera tax, and of course the obligatory guide.

The porters would be paid on our return, and a crowd of men gathered for selection. This was a noisy, and not altogether pleasant affair, as those not selected did not hide their disappointment. I made certain I could recognise the porter who had been allotted to me. "He will stay with you all the time," I was told.

Very early next morning, as we started to walk through the banana trees and mealie fields of the foothills, I was surprised to see my belongings speed past me on the back of a small child. Apparently, portering is sub-contracted!

At about the tenth river crossing, many hours later, we paused for slices of pineapple. Our porters were nowhere to be seen. A grunting and sighing noise came through the undergrowth. The jungle was so thick I could not see more than a few feet. Around the corner came a black pig, tied with a rope on its front trotter. A small boy held the other end. The pig collapsed into the river and let the icy waters run over its body, oblivious to the pulls of the boy.

We saw the pig again as we wearily approached the hut for the first night. It was lying on its back, slit up the middle, its innards on display. The porters had a fire blazing, and looked well pleased with the thought of dinner. Our dinner had to be made, and even our best cook couldn't make the dehydes taste like the picture on the box. And it wasn't the turn for our best cook to prepare dinner anyway . . .

A Dutch party were in the hut, waiting for a number of their group to recover. Altitude sickness had taken its toll. Rations were running out – I had never before seen twelve people have only custard for breakfast.

Luckily we had a doctor in our group. He looked at the invalids, bemoaning his lack of a stethoscope, then pronounced his expert medical opinion to the Dutch leader. "They must get down the mountain as soon as possible."

The next day was long and hard, but the weather remained fine. The views through gaps in the vegetation were splendid. Below – the plain. Ahead – the jagged, toothy mountains covered in snow. In the reign of the Pharaohs, Ptolemy had called them "The Mountains of the Moon", and succeeding generations have not found a better name.

The second night's hut was minus half the floor. Not too much of a problem until darkness fell. Then the holes disappeared in the lakes of blackness around the feeble, flickering light of our candles.

The next day's trek was the hardest exercise I have ever undertaken. The trees gave way to an evil forest of giant twenty-foot high heather. Yes, I know. I didn't believe it either. Imagine the gnarled, twisted branches of heather, average height twenty feet. They have been growing since the mountains began. As they die, their offspring force up through the fallen trunks. We climbed up, almost vertically, over twisting roots and branches. There was no discernible ground. Sometimes a rock would thrust up, but between the roots were large holes. Thick bright green Spanish moss covered everything. It hung from the branches, covered the path, changed the light to green. Water collecting on the moss makes black mud from the mouldering wood. It pulled at my boots and held them as I tried to pull myself up three feet over fallen trunks. Three solid hours of agony.

As if someone had drawn a line across the forest with a ruler, it all suddenly ended. Ahead was a slope covered in giant lobelia, lush growth, and bright butterflies which flew between tall succulents. I wondered if the butterflies lived their entire life at this altitude. Their short lives would surely be over before they could fly down to ground level.

The path ran up a gentle slope covered in dense ground-covering vegetation. I collapsed on it and studied the view. Below, way below, was a lake. Its waters were green. A hint of wispy white crossed the

The Ruwenzoris – 'Mountains of the Moon' – in Zaire. *(The Flowers of The Ruwenzoris)*

The 'mighty Rejang' at Kapit in Sarawak. *(Anything But Noodles)*

lake, followed a short while later by another. I stood up, and to my concern I could see far below clouds starting to swirl up the mountain. I had not gone through this agony only to have the view hidden by clouds. I forged on: it was now a race between me and the clouds. Only they were not wearing heavy, uncomfortable mud-caked boots.

The thing about hills that is so unfair is that as soon as you get to the top, you find it is not the top at all: there is always another ridge ahead. And so it was here. Down, then up again. My neck started to ache from turning around to see how the clouds were performing. Already the plain and foothills were hidden, and every now and then a wispy tendril would swirl up past me like smoke from a giant's cigarette.

Then I was walking along a ridge like the blade of a blunt knife. Stumpy bushes with thorns pulled at my trousers as I stumbled on granite outcrops. At last, a soft earth mound. It was so steep I did not have the energy to walk up but went on all fours, my pack banging on my back. My boots slipped on the soil, and my fingers grabbed twigs and plants for a grip. I could hear my breath panting in my chest.

Suddenly, there was the hut. On a grassy promontory with the glacier behind it, shining so brightly in the sun that it made my eyes screw up to look at it. And the hut was surrounded by pretty pink and white flowers. Little smudges of colour in the vast panorama in front of me.

Well, I beat the clouds by thirty minutes. Time to devour the view, and some nuts, raisins and a pineapple. Three young, disgustingly fit and healthy Americans passed us while we stretched out exhausted. They had been camping on the glacier. They spent three months each year climbing in different countries. They said the walk up to this point was tougher than "Kili". (Mount Kilimanjaro exerts a strange spell over all who see it; they are never able to utter it's name in full.)

I had done it. Me, overweight, under-exercised office worker. I was pleased, proud almost, but my overwhelming thought was "Never Again!"

And what a pity about the pink and white flowers. The mountain huts had probably last been maintained by the Belgians, and the earth closet next to this hut had filled up many years ago. The flowers were left by visitors, by courtesy of Dixcel and Andrex and their kind.

Local fiesta in Peru, with accompanying band. (*Triple Alliance*)

PHILIP CLARKE

Triple Alliance

I do not recall how much my memories of that night-time journey were the creation of fitful dreams or the stuff of actuality. The blackness of the night and my own fears were real enough as the lights of the bus probed the landscape, revealing steep escarpments and the outlines of vertical cliffs. Sometimes, peering over the side of the bus, I caught sight of the ghostly white caps of Pacific rollers coming to spit their fury at a continent. The bus swept down the hills and then ground its way up another hilltop through a succession of sandy switchbacks. I kept thinking of the drunken Cary Grant in *North by Northwest,* as he strove to bring his car under control. Was our driver chewing coca leaves, as so many long distance drivers did in Peru, to ease the burdens of an eight-hour journey? I looked around the bus at the crumpled figures managing some sleep. Two rows in front of me a Japanese man slumped against a girl with a shock of auburn curls. A strange couple, I thought.

The first tendrils of light spawned a mist, which hung over the desert. In my half-sleep I thought the sand was snow for it had the thick texture of water-colour paper. It felt very cold.

The sun was already bright as silver on our arrival in Arequipa, a large city but untouched by ugly tall buildings. A colonial city with a sunny disposition. I found my bag and smiled at the Japanese and the girl with auburn curls. I produced my guidebook as an invitation to treat.

"Which hotel?" I asked. We introduced ourselves. The girl was German: a student dressed in ten different colours but unsmiling. Kazuo, a tall peering Japanese, was smiling, but smiling with the fixity of the nervous. There was an instant unspoken bargain struck. Travelling alone in Peru was a nerve-racking business. We would find a hotel together. One minute later, as we strode through the streets of Arequipa to the racing pace set by Regina, we found that our plans for the next week were almost identical.

"It would be nice to travel together," I ventured.

Over breakfast in our modest traveller's *pension,* with its sunlit courtyard full of cardinal red geraniums, we traded our identities in English, which was the only language we understood in common. The petty deceits that circumscribe our contact with other people become redundant in the fleeting moments one has with other travellers. Family bereavement had bred in Regina a sense of independence and toughness, akin to isolation. At eighteen she had felt the call to move away from home, a state of affairs accepted with stoicism by her mother. She had been travelling for three months in the Americas, but a recent illness, she confessed, had made her very vulnerable. Regina had a very clear idea what she wanted to see and to experience, and a buoyant belief that nothing bad could befall her.

Kazuo always expected the worst. He was travelling around the world and was sceptical of everybody and everything. His itinerary was frenetic, as notions of travel seemed to be based on seeing and recording a certain number of spectacular sights. His schedule gave him security, I smugly conceded, but given his language difficulties and the Japanese ambivalence towards travel, he was brave enough as it was. When he returned home, he hoped to secure employment where he could take three weeks of holiday every third year.

"We Japanese are an undeveloped people," he lamented. "I have brought discomfort to my parents," he added even more wistfully.

We spent three days in Arequipa. I learnt to adapt to Regina's pace and to Kazuo's sharp cries of pleasure at seeing any Japanese goods. As nearly every car in Peru was Japanese, these cries would punctuate any long silences. Conversation, under these circumstances, is a bit of an effort, as bonhomie can be taken only so far before familiarity makes it both superfluous and a little ridiculous. We did, however, share one common characteristic – we were all introverts, but that was about as far as it went. For a start, we must have looked an unlikely assortment: a German hippy with flowers decorating her trousers; a tall Japanese continually grimacing and emitting cries; and myself, wrapped against the sun and locked into my duty to promote conversation.

The train to Puno is regarded as one of the most spectacular rail journeys in the world. It is also one of the most dangerous. The guidebooks all suggest that there is an eighty per cent chance of having something stolen. The station at Arequipa has a particularly unpleasant reputation for bag-slashing, petty theft and daylight robbery. I remember sleeping fitfully, working out how I would deal with my attackers and protect my companions, but these plans were unnecessary. We took a taxi into the station, where it rapidly became apparent that the spectre of the bad guys hanging around in gangs like *West Side Story* extras was the stuff of dreams. Instead, traditionally-dressed women waddled along the platform carrying mountainous baskets.

The train pulled its way up onto the altiplano with its stunning emptiness and its snow-capped mountains beyond. Whatever pleasure one has in the newness of it all, the harshness soon becomes apparent. For the spectator the coruscating sodium light and the pounding of one's temples from the 15,000-foot altitude are not conducive to appreciation. For the Indian there is a bleakness that their bright clothing cannot efface – dun-coloured landscapes, an absence of trees and shrubs, and a piercing wind setting up miniature whirlwinds which bob across the tableau. Three or four adobe houses cluster near the railway, where a dog may raise himself to give sporting chase to the train. In fixing such a picture in time, one had mood in plenty but no focal point – no dominant feature that would lead the eyes into the rest of the scene. Puno, a frontier town in both senses, on the shores of Lake Titicaca had both mood and focal point.

All through Puno, women, with hair plaited in pig-tails and hats perched uneasily on the crown of their heads, sported themselves under great bundles of cloth. I suppose the town must be the knitting capital of the world, for at every turn these women pursue you to sell pullovers, socks and ponchos. You are invited to try on a whole array of richly hued garments. "Ah Señor, jumper," they would mew in the sing-song style of imitation subservience. If you want to dress like a canary, this is the place for you. Regina was in her element here, and rather unheeding of male boredom.

When we arrived, it was dark. Regina grabbed the key for the last room in the cheapest hotel in town. Fortunately it had three beds in it, but that was about as far as comfort went; it was small and cold, but for a dollar a day it was acceptable. Our *ménage à trois* did not have the sporting connotations that the term suggests. The marriage of convenience was simply that. It was difficult enough to sort out three lots of clothes, to adjust our points of demarcation and to ward off the cold without having to worry about potential embarrassments. National characteristics, as I like to think of them, rather than mere idiosyncracies, were paraded for each of us to see. In the Japanese world to my right, everything was arranged "just so".

To each object its allotted place – the pad for origami, the box for shaving gear, a diary full of pasted tickets, along with paste, Sellotape and pencils in another bag, the calculator and a camera in another compartment. Clothes were placed as if they had been left by a valet. The detail of routine brought order into the unpredictable world. On coming into our bedroom, Kazuo's first act would be to close the window, whilst Regina's would be to open it again. At such times Kazuo took on the muted solemnity of an afflicted Thurber husband. He lived his life by a different code. "I could not marry your Western girls," he once confided to me.

And to my left was Regina, who shattered my preconceptions about German order. Clothes were thrown everywhere, and added to with fresh purchases of woollen garments from the market stalls. Where she did conform more clearly to the national stereotype was in the continual use of the imperative. "We vill be having a shower this morning – yes?"

"We vill," I sang back. However, we both shared a fascination for the quiet rituals of the Japanese – the gentle massage of his face and the toning of each muscle as he got up, the clasping of his hands in prayer at the end of each meal – embodying all the gentility that our harsher Anglo-Saxon cultures had lost.

The train journey to Cuzco, the imperial capital of the Incas, was wearisome – like passing through an endless corridor in which small boys kept hitting your head with books. We stopped at a series of villages and small towns, all with the same harshness of colour. At one stop, where we spent no more than a minute, a middle-aged man slipped out of a doorway and leant against the adjacent wall. A small child approached him with a bottle in one hand and money in the other, but dropped the bottle at the moment of transfer. The man cursed and staggered away, leaving the child standing stock still. The train moved off.

We had begun to get to know each other, and with this understanding came the explanations of what it was like to be German, Japanese and English. We teased each other about our idiosyncrasies and our pretensions. Kazuo admitted that hard work blinded many Japanese to the potential of life. On his travels he had felt more at home in Germany than in any other country. He had found the British rather disdainful. Regina spoke with pride about her love for Germany and about her irritation with questions concerning Hitler. Little failures were confessed and hopes expressed. The common chords of isolation and uncertainty were gently touched. I had the advantage of language and taught Kazuo idioms. "What is this 'bright-eyed and bushy-tailed' that I am this morning?" he kept muttering.

"'Danger of homosexual rape' the guidebook says," I read out, as we got up and started planning our day. Kazuo reached for his dictionary, found the appropriate words and shook his head in dismay. "Very strange, very strange." We would then march off to find breakfast, making it clear to Regina that muesli and yoghurt were not our idea of breakfast; but she always won because she knew precisely what she wanted. Inadequately fortified, we would follow her to see some imposing Incan ruin with its perfectly-shaped rectangles of rock fitted together with mortar. Regina would lie in the sun catching the atmosphere, while Kazuo and I would trot around every nook and cranny in case we missed anything. "No rape today – very good day," Kazuo would comment and then slyly smile.

I watched them pack early on our final morning together. Regina and Kazuo were continuing on to Macchu Picchu before Regina returned home, while I was going into the interior. Our farewells were brief as we noted the happiness of the week and the fact that we were sorry to be parting. Yes, of course, we would try and meet again. I heard them close the front door and move out into the darkness.

MARION LEEPER

BLANK CASSETTES

The apartment looks both ways: from one balcony you can see the orange roofs of the old town, and the other looks out over the harbour, over the clusters of fishing boats and wealthy dinghies in the Puerto Mahon at the foot of the cliff, the blinking white apartment blocks in Villa Carlos on the right, and, opposite, the eighteenth-century prison (no longer functional, therefore picturesque) on the island opposite.

Last year my father spent most of his day looking at this view. He would potter out here in the morning and laboriously roll down the blind to keep the sun off the Chinese rugs. Then he would see to the plants, bougainvillea, cacti, geraniums – very occasionally there would be a weed to pull up – and sit down with a book on his knee, (Homer, or Agatha Christie).

By then the sun no longer streaks the water with blinding paths of early morning light: the view seems bleached and flattened. And at midnight, as I write on sunburnt knees, the harbour is only a black shape between the streetlights. An improbable Georgian building picked out in violent terracotta is floodlit; so is the door of the discotheque, carved out of a cave in the cliff. Insectoid mopeds, with pillions and no helmets, are buzzing round the roundabout and down the hill.

Two men with a van have opened a manhole and are doing something to the drains. The street sweeper has just been, and the dustbin lorry has stopped outside for a drink at the bar opposite. The nightlife is just beginning: the disco's last customers are still being thrown out when the first of the children get up at six.

Last year there was a ship, a large rusty tanker right in the middle of the harbour. Everyone made a great drama out of it. Coming back from distant beaches for tea with my father (little dry biscuits and China tea with lemon) we would rush in and ask: "The ship! Is it still there?" It always was: the excitement faded when we discovered it had been abandoned by its owners, probably along with its crew.

This year the flat is empty when we arrive. On the intercom, instead of my father's cross voice which he kept for machinery and naughty children, there is only silence. In the shop next door, where I go to buy a picnic and to ask in phrase-book Spanish after the friends we are holidaying with, they recognise me, to my delight. The shop is run by Ophelia. The name hardly prepares one for the small practical woman, her expression severe with the worry of running a shop and bringing up a young family. Her sister Mandi – when we first came a mooning, sulky girl saving up to marry her *novio* – this year has smiles all over her face and a three-month-old baby with almond eyes and beautiful long thin feet.

"Esta bien sua madre?"

"No, no esta aqui."

They are very sorry that she is so ill and, unsure how to resolve the misunderstanding, I say lamely *"Esta mexor . . ."* and go off with my bread and wine and ham.

We soon find our friends, and the flat is given over to the noise of children, having sand washed out of them and food put into them. (We eat very Spanish – *sobrasada,* tomatoes, fish fingers.)

This year the island is full to bursting with tourists. Everywhere is surlier and more expensive. In front of the magnificent palmshaded Moorish palace which is Ciudadella town hall, I am buttonholed by a Scotsman who wants to know whether there are any traffic wardens likely to book him, and how to work the lock on his hired car. In one of the harbour-front restaurants at Fornells (where, it is rumoured, King Juan Carlos was turned away because he hadn't booked) a large lady with heaving shoulders creates a magnificent scene. We watch spellbound as she stalks up to the bar to shout at the manager. "You don't speak English, you made us wait an hour for our food, you even got our drinks wrong and now it's raining on us!" And she sweeps out, bearing her husband before her and holding her handbag like a cosh.

My father also used to make little trips at lunchtime to restaurants by the sea. They would order very plain food – all he could eat – and my mother would say "Isn't this lovely! Eggs taste so much nicer in Spain."

On the beach, miles of sand are punctuated by tall white hotels and gleaming new apartment blocks (meanwhile no-one comes to see or buy my mother's flat). Along the narrow strip of wet sand at the edge of the water stroll the holidaymakers, one foot higher than the other, their shoulders kaleidescopic pinks and browns. The English are identifiable by their puce colour, or by their high-pitched Sloane voices calling from sailboard to sailboard.

This seasonal invasion is nothing new to the Menorquins. The French and the British both invaded Menorca over the last 200 years: the French invented mayonnaise here, but they seem to have taken it away with them – at least we have not encountered it. The British left huge gobbets of imposing Georgian architecture, like the barracks, now painted purple but still in use, and they taught the Menorquins how to make gin, which they pronounce with difficulty but continue to make in fishermen's (smugglers?) caves hollowed out of the cliff along the seafront.

We spend every spare moment on the beach. The baby finds it difficult to tell where the sea begins and the land ends. He finally toddles into the water and throws himself in face forward with howls of delight. Six Spanish ladies in black bikinis notice his antics and his blond hair and follow him round, *"Che guapo . . . how pretty . . . muy hombre"*. He is very pleased with his impromtu court and yells when we take him off for lunch and an unsuccessful siesta in a nest of cockroaches underneath a pine tree.

My father wasn't always confined to the balcony. For a long time he went every day to the *estanco* round the corner to buy the local paper, though his walking was shaky: my mother used to stand on the balcony and watch him surreptitiously in case he fell over. In the town he had special friends he would go and chat to: like the old lady in the shop that sold fifty different sorts of olives, out of big jars. Sometimes he went with my mother to the children's shop to help choose beautiful and expensive clothes for the grandchildren. The shopkeeper was also the manager of the football team (you can see the football stadium, nearly always empty, from our balcony) and large football players could be found among the tiny dresses, come to tell her all their troubles.

Once my mother lost him and scoured the streets for him, thinking he'd dropped dead. In fact he'd sneaked out for a haircut, but the barber had shut up shop for the siesta and he and my father were drinking a glass of wine together.

We've turned our backs on the town: it's too far for the children to walk. We do venture into the white-tiled cloister of the large church nearby, where they hold the covered market daily. Vegetables in lavish piles and dairy stalls with all sorts of sausage hanging in bunches and as many potent local cheeses: we are seduced by the names and colours and buy far too much – *marmelata, sobrasada, mantequilla, berenjenas . . .*

In the open space in the centre is the fish market. A matron in black with wonderful red hair, in charge of one of the stalls, calls out with every other word to "Jesu" and "Maria" – my parents used to point her out proudly as a retired madam, "and that hair is definitely a wig!"

When we finally get into the town centre it is fiesta day. The streets are empty, the gift shops have wire mesh over their windows, and tourists sit nervously opposite their suitcases in the cafés. It is changeover day at Gatwick. Little girls in identical white dresses, looking frighteningly like the rows of porcelain dolls locked away inside the deserted gift shops, are coming out of the cathedral after their first communion and posing for photographs on the steps with beaming grandmothers and aunts.

Soon it is time for us to lug suitcases back to the airport, to England and the remains of the cold wet summer. The flat is eventually sold with all its furnishings, including, in the corner cupboard, the cassettes which, months before he died, my father inscribed in his shaky handwriting "Mozart piano concerto . . . Beethoven sonata . . ." Unfortunately, because he wasn't good at working machinery, when you try and play them they are completely blank.

FRANCES ROBERTSON

HIDDEN RIVERS

As I climbed up out of the station the street stretched away uphill, shining under the lights like an old trouser seat. There were houses everywhere and scraggy trees, but I couldn't see a pub anywhere. Thin drizzle peppered the thirsty pavements and I realised this was a hopeful start; I'd found a real, if repellent, suburb in an elusive city. I was standing in Salusbury Road, in Queen's Park, in London.

Some of the shadowy nature of London is that one feels it ought to be well known. Anyone who can read can know London; from Dick Whittington to witty Dickens and beyond, every view is veiled with reference.

This time, in my search for the real London, my only literature was the A-Z street guide and the Underground map. But even the Underground, although picturesque, is not suitable for an *entire* holiday, although I am convinced that many travellers are diverted to this stratum. It is so easy to bolt down a hole into the roaring maze and follow the red, the brown, or the stripey thread of the map; following that thread along the acrid windy galleries and moving stairs becomes the real adventure. To be sure, you can pop up at the V & A or Madame Tussauds, but how are they connected except by this bloodless Tube filled with the sound of sighs? There is no real evidence that these sights are on the same planet, never mind in the same city.

On this holiday I was determined to discover what else was possible. I had a pretty good chance on two counts: I was to stay in Queen's Park, an inkwell into which no writer's pen I knew had ever dipped, and I was on a working holiday, to study costume cutting. Between the artisans' dwellings and the crash of shears on calico I was out on my own, gathering raw experience as the baleen whale sucks in slime. That was my plan.

I soon found Queen's Park to be inhospitable; intended by philanthropists as a suburb to encourage workers to be thrifty, not thirsty, there are no pubs at all and scarcely any other comforts.

But Soho, where I tubed to my studies, is the opposite. Sandwiched between the drinking establishments are crammed shops for food, sex, clothes of every description. It is a black sun to the asteroids of the entertainment industry. To a seamstress from the provinces like me, this area bulges with every conceivable oddity and commodity such as iridescent diamond buttons and leather knickers. In my lunch breaks I bought bread and cheese in Brewer Street, and what *lovely* bread and cheese – rubbery Italian bread, salty *pecorino* and mammoth olives as large and pungent as ancient eggs.

The Association of British Theatre Technicians in Great Pulteney Street, where I pursued my studies, is a kind of temple to artifice, dedicated to the mechanisms of theatrical illusion. One steps through a plain door off the street and up the wooden stairs. There are offices and a small lecture room, the ceiling of which is crammed for teaching with more lanterns than could light a small theatre. I imagine a weekend lighting course with the enthusiastic lads and girls rushing up and down steps, focusing the lenses.

But this weekend is for costume cutting and we are all girls; pinning, measuring and sewing, lashed on by our two teachers. There is so little time and so much to learn. There are twelve of us from all parts zf the country – I came down by bus from Scotland. Only the thirst for knowledge will ever force me to travel that way again, but it's the cheapest when you're unemployed. There's another girl there as skint as I am, Izzie from Oxford. She's wearing a leather mini-skirt which unzips entirely into shreds and is quite obviously pilfered from some bygone production.

Izzie's made a special corset for one of our teachers and laces her into it at the end of the day. The peristalsis of sprung steel and canvas half swallows her down and displays a heroine of the *belle époque;* tiny waist and huge trembling bosom. Shrieks! – Is there a man looking in from across the road?

Then we close the windows, consult the maps and leave our dressmakers' dummies standing in the darkening room. Twelve of them, in their calico finery.

That evening my hosts were to sing in a concert in Highgate, and I might join them if I was early enough. By the time I'd won through to Archway Station (which sounded cryptic) and started up Highgate Hill (which did not) it was too late, the concert had already started. But by this time my A–Z had become like one of those magic painting books children have, where a few strokes with a wet brush make the colours appear between the lines. London was growing up around my eyes and under my exhausted feet. To colour in some more of the network of streets and names I would walk right over the hill and down to Highgate Station.

After a steep climb I came to a park, where the ponds lie in levels under the hilltop and trees hang in curtains above. The smell of earth and new leaves rose up as the rain dropped in rings. Water gleamed in veils on every bank and I soon realised this was not a passive wetness, but that the whole area was alive and springing with moisture.

Later, back at home, I described where I had been to my hosts. Where does that water *go to,* I wondered?

"Aha!" cried my hostess, flourishing a book out of the shelves.

"You have observed the source of one of *The Lost Rivers of London.* [This is the title of the book, by Nicholas Barton.] You were in Water-low Park, and right across the hill (which lies like a soggy sponge on a draining-board), through Highgate Ponds to Hampstead, spring up streams that feed the river Fleet, once an important tributary of the Thames and sometime known as the River of Wells. It is now a gigantic sewer culverted away underground and pours into the Thames below Blackfriars Bridge." She paused for breath and resumed:

"To where Fleet-ditch with disemboguing streams
Rolls the large Tribute of dead dogs to Thames".

This, I discover, is a quotation from Alexander Pope's *The Dunciad.* After this impromptu lecture I took the book to bed and coloured in courses of the hidden rivers in my A–Z with a blue felt-tip pen.

I was fascinated. The water I had seen today was now running down from Kentish Town to Pentonville, Clerkenwell and Holborn, gurgling secretly under houses and unknown to the sleepers above except the lucky few (as I read) with observation trapdoors in their cellars.

I told myself there was no real mystery to it; that any great city needs, and pollutes, water on a massive scale. But all the next day, in the lecture room, and on the bus home with a stiff neck and a bad temper, a trickle grew and grew in my inward ears into a silently roaring flood which swept away all I had known before.

The imprisoned rivers vaulted over with streets and houses seemed to me the most real thing I had found on my journey.

ANITA PELTONEN

ON WINTER'S CUSP

The trains don't go past the Arctic Circle in Finland. The tracks stop at Rovaniemi, latitude $66\frac{1}{2}$ degrees N, which was burnt to the ground by the Germans in 1944. Viewed from the air, the rebuilt city forms a reindeer's head with antlers, and is known as the gateway to Lappland.

At the point where the last major northbound road intersects the Circle, there is a village set up as Santa Claus's North Pole. This may be Finland's only rigged tourist attraction. Concorde flies there once a year from London, but Santa seekers don't stay the night. We drove, as our destination was the heart of Lappland, way beyond Rovaniemi. It was the very first week in September; the days would still outlast the nights even if the flattening of the sun's arc foretold the imminent arrival of day-long nights.

The Lapps are said to be telepathic. They communicate intricately through the beating of drums. Saami, the Lappish tongue, is incomprehensible to the Finn. Its use is so localised that one family will usually not understand another. They survive by herding reindeer.

My companion was Finnish, but Lappland is a remote destination even by a Finn's standards. Lapps have never been known to leave their encampments for the bright lights of the south. Their isolation is utter. Taking a westerly route northbound, we edged the Baltic all the way up. The nearly empty road was hugged by a strangulating tunnel of pine trees so that only once, when a bridge crossed a marsh, did we glimpse water. Just short of the Swedish border we turned inland toward Rovaniemi at a harbour town called Ii. Its name seemed an ululating cry of escape from the tunnel of pines.

Beyond Rovaniemi the birches and pines thinned to yield a brightness that jangled after the dimness of the forests. The image of a land inhabited by an unreachable race of people and cruel extremes of dark, light and elements fell away. Lappland seemed instead to have been touched by the gentlest of hands.

The softly tilting hills went on out of sight, gold, purple and rust. The colour came from Arctic birch, which, above the timberline, drops out of tree form and crawls up the hillsides in a thickly netted ground cover. This far north the autumn colours flare early.

Inari, an enormous lake at the crown of Finland, was our north-ernmost stop. An errant Soviet test missile splashed down in it two winters ago, making world headlines (and causing thermal shock to a team of journalists called in from Saudi Arabia to cover it). The lake was black as obsidian and still as ice, reflecting the gathering darkness. We rented a tiny cabin very near Inari's shores. A river across the way fed into the lake. We walked through the twilit, lichen-spurred woods. The ground was carpeted with wild cloudberries. When we doubled back along the track we had come on, it looked so unfamiliar that we almost abandoned it. We had to attribute it to something – Lappdust.

We ate at a small hunting lodge attached to the group of cabins we were staying in, and then went walking again. The light remained as at deep dusk. There was a dim blaze in the east where the sun had gone down. The rising brick-red moon waxed full strength; then, in less than a quarter of an hour, glimmered to opalescent; it was huge as a picnic plate. The silence was near absolute. One could imagine hearing the hiss and swirl of the planets.

We decided then to take in Inari. Planted on the deck of one of the summer cruise boats, we leaned way back and searched for our bear-ings in the unfamiliar, northerly alignments of the constellations. Half an hour passed. The moon moved at startling speed across the sky, its progress marked against spearheaded pinetops. Nothing moved but a single fish, which skimmed just below the lake's surface but did not rupture it.

But then: the vacuum broke. No strident howl or cry could have created the same effect. Out of the felt blue woods, startling softly so that it seeped into rather than shattered the silence, came the most un-expected of sounds – grunting, rooting, and belching.

Wild boar were possible in Lappland, but the movement of these animals was slow, shuffling. There were clearly several of them. Ex-cept for shy, smallish brown bears and the rare lynx, there weren't any large, harmful animals here. And we were on a boat. I couldn't picture any of these leaping through the air onto a boat. But still . . . We squatted down to peer through the cabin window. Moments passed; they were clearly approaching the bank. My friend said "Now stand up," but I didn't.

"What?" I said.

"You don't want to miss this."

I stood.

Into the searing blue-white pyramid of moonbeam that cut through the near group of trees glided four grandly-antlered creatures. Two kept heads to the ground; two de-furred the trees of their periwinkles of lichen. They were bottle-nosed, which may account for the grunting noises which could be heard at full tilt now. Only when we angled around to get a fuller view did we see that the two reindeer standing at the back were albino. Pure white with bleached antlers, they were a negativity of light, as the Lappish summer day is an absence of night.

Just as the vapours of a dream fade, they moved, after a time, white on white, slowly out of vision into the throat of the woods.

Afterword: people don't look when they cross the road in Lappland because usually no-one's coming. Neither do the reindeer. Used to human contact and traffic, they often plod into the road and linger, seeming to know that the damage they would do to you/your car upon contact is awesome.

The following day we were heading off on a spur road toward Norway. We hadn't gone more than a minute when a sizeable group of reindeer, including (the same?) two albinos, ambled across. I stopped the car and, armed with telephoto lens, followed them into the woods. On cloven hooves, they moved a lot faster than I did. I didn't realise how long I followed them, I was so intent on getting a photo (made the more difficult because they were never still).

I had snapped just one when the Lappish forest was invaded by a wholly un-native voice. The reindeer turned lazily toward it, then (in disgust, I imagined) headed off. My friend, stranded at the car and certain the Lappdust had gotten me so that I couldn't find my way back, had bolted a Frank Zappa cassette into the player and turned the volume up to lethal. It was an excellent homing device. The photo turned out fairly well.

I think I'd like to go back some time when Lappland is six feet under snow, and see the Northern lights. I wonder if the Lapps have an explanation for them that can rival Canada's Baffin Island Eskimos, who believe the glimmering, pitching lights are caused by the gods' children playing football with the umbilical cords of stillborn babies.

TANIA BROWN

MEXICAN UNDERGROUND

I need a new passport. Of course it won't be ready for three days, so I decide to look into the visas I need for the Central American countries I want to travel through. The man at the British Embassy gives me the address of the Honduran Embassy – ninth floor of the Edificio San Antonio, and I press my way through the crowded city to Insurgentes metro station.

There's still enormous earthquake damage in Mexico City. Buildings lean at extreme angles; stairways hang off walls and lead to nowhere. Hotels and office blocks split perfectly in two stand empty and crumbling. Most are waiting to be pulled down and the Mexicans have hardly started. But underground the metro is unaffected. It's surprisingly fast, clean, efficient and extremely cheap. Two pence to any destination, recently raised 2,000 per cent to keep pace with inflation.

The platforms are brightly lit. But cramped. I've never seen so many people in such a tiny space. More arrive every second. The train rushes in, preceded by a wind that relieves some of the ghastly claustrophobia. The doors open. Passengers fight to get out but lose the battle and the crowd surges in. I imagine passengers being packed into the furthest corners of the train, never to emerge, and decide this is why the carriages get packed tighter and tighter throughout the day. The carriages are solid with people. There are plugs of people at each entrance, all still trying to get in. It's impossible. They prevent the doors from shutting and slow the whole business down. More people arrive. They join the semi-circular crowds at each door to heave and push as if they, too, can somehow catch the train.

I expect a long delay. But the Mexican railways are used to the Mexican people and the doors turn out to be unexpectedly powerful. With a snap they are shut. Where the doors meet with rubber jaws a few morsels of people remain trapped. The crowd sorts this out by dragging arms and legs with great friction through the black rubber jaws. Those caught halfway-in they jam tightly into the carriage by stamping on them vertically. Or by charging sideways to repeatedly ram them with their shoulders. Thereafter, whenever I travel on the metro, I can recognise people who have been through this treatment by the muddy footprints on their clothes and the two black lines down their arms.

The train rushes off, people stuffed tightly along its length. Dotted over the glass windows and doors are irregular shaped flat areas of flesh, each with the faint condensation of sweat around it, as passengers' noses, arms, mouths and cheeks are pressed hard against the glass. Gargoyle expressions glare out in pain from the crush. I'm glad I missed that train.

The next crush. A man had his head stuck at waist level in the crowd. He can't pull it out. He's trying to reach something he's dropped. A passport by my feet. I see him straining but he's locked solid. I execute a policeman's knee bend and lower my body vertically in the crowd until I can reach it for him. When I surface he's pressing his way out of the door. *"Señor!"* I call to him and reach out over the crowd. But he's gone. I look at the passport in my hand. It's my own! Suddenly the crush relaxes as nine thieves tumble out onto the platform and disappear.

At every station traders jump on and off with bags full of things to sell. Peanuts, Chiclets, hard-boiled sweets. Snakes and ladders games. Religious tracts. An old man with 'Kojak' lollipops (six for a hundred pesos) tells us he's offering them at this price as a "promotion". He walks the length of the carriage, lollipops arranged in an attractive pattern in his fist, announcing the advantages of his product in a loud monotone. No-one buys a thing. Next, an urchin, small notebooks and address books in pink and blue, arranged in a fan. He pauses to turn one over, back and forth. He flicks through the pages and displays the impressive strength of the cardboard covers to the disinterested, captive audience. No-one buys a thing. A blind old man plays harmonica. Token notes really, hardly a tune. A dirty kid with crew cut wanders round in search of donations for his talent.

Hidalgo Station. The daylight dazzles. I push my way through the thronging crowd and stop at a post office. People sit on the steps outside selling lottery tickets, newspapers, envelopes, all shouting and pulling the hem of my shirt for business. Inside it is grey and cool. There are no scales but my letters are passed to a man in the corner. "Air mail?" Yes. He judges the weight in his hand by lightly throwing them up and down, then picks out stamps for each one. I have no doubt he is spot on. I've seen it before, in the markets, where traders pick out different weights of produce with uncanny accuracy. People pass him more mail. He judges each one. I wonder if he's calibrated to do parcels as well?

I feel very sorry for people who have faces that make me feel sad. Faces that are humble and honest, not mean, shrewd and hard. Like the old man playing accordion in the doorway of the café. He looks so expectantly towards his audience as he plays, expecting to see delight. As a father would look to the happiness on his child's face at Christmas. But his tune is always the same, and played jerkily in disjointed pieces. His foot is bandaged with a dirty rag. It makes him limp so painfully I wince, but the expectant smile never leaves his face. I finish my bottle of Sangria and follow him. He stands at the doorway of the next café, then the next one. People ignore him so I give him fifty pesos.

Some of the women in the *tortilleria* are dressed in flouncy pink, red and white Spanish dresses. Hooped earrings, heavy make-up. Red lipstick, long eyelashes, black mascara. High-heeled shoes, piled up hairdos, with curls around the temples. Yet they're working in extreme heat – sweating gallons. They hump dough around, do heavy work on the machines. They're tough with well-developed arm muscles. Like men in drag.

Trucks swerve and dodge down the road belching thick, foul-tasting diesel fumes. Most are unsilenced and the noise hurts my ears. The front bumpers are personalised in the way the drivers see themselves; "El Fury", "Rambo", "Prisonero del Bar". It takes fifteen minutes to cross the road. Around the corner is the Edificio San Antonio. I walk up to the doorway. It is locked. Then I realise the building has only seven floors. Vertical cracks run up the face of the building. Rubble from collapsed floors pours out of paneless windows. As I sit on a park bench opposite to eat some sandwiches, lethargic workmen are slowly pulling the earthquake-damaged building to pieces. Britain's diplomatic ties with the Hondurans, I decided, could not be close.

MARGARET HENDERSON

ONE DAY ALONG THE GOLDEN ROAD

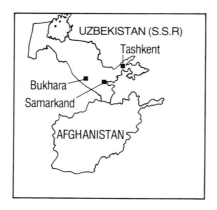

It was only on the way to Samarkand, the real pearl of ancient Central Asia (now the pearl of the Soviet Socialist Republic of Uzbekistan). But the memories of that day in little Bukhara are more vivid, more persistent, and looking back I think I understand why, through the centuries, merchants and pilgrims and assorted adventurers, guided by nothing but the stars, were prepared to brave the Red Sand Desert, the Celestial Mountains, the look-outs on the Tower of Death and very likely the Black Pit of vipers and vermin for a look at the fabulous, forbidden town.

They say that only two Christians defiled Bukhara with their infidel gaze in the 400 years before 1840. That was the year Captain Connolly of the Bengal Light Cavalry crawled out of the pit with his flesh in tatters, to have his head cut off in the ceremonial courtyard for his pains.

I expect we must have crossed the desert, too, but it had been bedtime, mine at least, before we got airborne from Tashkent. Missed the desert stars, was my first thought as I woke to soft music. (Fly Aeroflot and you take off and land to the sound of the balalaika.) But that was silly, because you never see stars from planes, not in my experience anyway.

At the tourist hotel Bokhoro (it's the only one so far) my new floor lady rose cheerfully from a snooze in her armchair beside the lift and fetched some lemon tea from the electric samovar along the corridor. She giggled behind a modest hand as she helped me out of my light jacket to show me how I'd been wearing it inside out. I laughed along with her, then found my bed and flopped into sleep again for what remained of the night.

I was late in the morning of course, and the best I could do was to accept the kind offer from the Americans travelling Intourist de luxe in a curtained limousine.

"Gee," ventured Herb from Kansas City at the Tower of Death. "I guess this little minaret here must be nearly as tall as that space rocket at our Cape Canaveral. The one they take your picture beside. I have one. A pic I mean. Ever been to Florida? Nice. Everything brand new."

The Kalyan Minaret was 900 years old, 148 feet high, held together by an ancient mortar based on camel's milk. Herb leaned back as far as he could without toppling over to get it all on ciné.

In use, it had been what you might call a multi-purpose minaret. From its slender summit they must have watched anxiously for Tamerlaine, back specially from his Persian conquests to drive the Golden Horde from the town. In the intervals without strife they would read the starry constellations for signs of peace or war. It was also a sort of desert lighthouse. Fires were lit to guide the camel-trains through sandstorms to the safety of the caravanserais within the crenellated city walls. From the same minaret, muezzins had made calls to prayer and red guards proclamations of Soviet power. On bazaar days, not so very long ago, they used to push up the inside stair-way and down from the top to a public death thieves, murderers, drunks, adulterers, seditionists and barren wives. That's how it got its second name, the Tower of Death.

The next building, the one with the majolica mosaics, was the Miri-Arab Madrasah, a seminary for the priesthood and the headquarters of the Spiritual Board of Moslems of Central Asia and Kazakhstan. Round the corner a couple of young fellows on scaffolding were shar-ing a joke as they restored the gold tracery on the old hospice for wandering dervishes.

For the Americans it was time for lunch de luxe. For me, the Lyabi-khauz which, according to local intelligence, was as good a place as I was likely to find for a bowl of green tea and kebabs. It was the old town centre, the watering hole, now a clear, terraced pool overlooked by the winter mosque and surrounded by *sofes* – divans set with low tables for food or chess.

Out of an acacia tree above my *sofe* a flock of little boys dropped down, hoping for a magic picture from my camera. Alas, it wasn't a Polaroid. I searched my bag for a souvenir. "Eenglish money," said the one with the biggest brown eyes, more mischievously than expec-tantly, I thought. The man from the next table had overheard. He was wearing an armband on his *khalat,* the traditional navy blue quilted coat of the Uzbeks which wouldn't look out of place in a London club as a smoking jacket.

"Please, Madame. They are not hungry. It is different now," he said. I could see they had a problem. At the crossroads of the Great Silk Route, the human instinct for trading has a heritage of thousands of years. I was relieved that stickers and postcards from home met with his approval, and theirs.

At the Ark citadel and residence of the emirs I discreetly infiltrated another English-speaking group of tourists with an excellent guide, Tatyana.

Time hadn't mellowed these emirs a bit. The last of them, one Abdul Said Mir Alim Khan, was as gifted in torture as any of his line. It was he who perfected the technique of the "sweet death", a concoction of boiling sugar poured down the throats of those of his harem who failed to please – women or boys, he wasn't too fussy. The boys travelled better when he fled before the Red Cavalry to a new life as a tea merchant, eventually, in Kabul, following a tip-off over the telephone still on display. That was in 1920.

On the way to the war memorial were the *taks* and the *tims,* the merchant domes and arcades of medieval times, still busy and in a fine state of preservation. The money-changers had gone, but not the hide-curers, nor the gold-thread embroiderers, the skull-cap sellers or the craftsmen in chased copper and alabaster. A sculptor worked on a terracotta statue of an Uzbek man wearing the *khalat* and baggy trousers stuck in high boots. The finely-modelled face was unmistakably Lenin's. Apprentices watched the masters at work or fetched glasses of water from the public drinks dispensers, fermented brown *kvass* or Pepsi-Cola (yes, Pepsi-Cola, it was written in Cyrillic script on the labels).

At the memorial to the Great Patriotic War, a large wedding party was stepping out of several decorated Ladas to leave the bridal bouquets at the tomb of the Unknown Soldier. Before I could ask for permission to snap them, they had pulled me into the family group and filled my arms with flowers. Two little sisters took charge of me as if I were a favourite auntie and shunted me around the memorial complex as the young photographer posed us like a real professional for his once-in-a-lifetime shots. At the end of the session the little girls patted me on the back as if I'd done rather well, considering.

It was noisy back at the hotel. Fireworks were popping to mark an announcement by Mr Gorbachev of a further moratorium on nuclear testing. They must have been hearing the music from the loudspeakers on the wall of the hotel's al fresco ice-cream parlour all over the town. And coming from the other side of the square was pop music from an open-air "youth café".

I sat down. Toddlers in the area with child-sized tables and chairs were attacking mountainous cream ices in three shades of pink. Our coach was back from the excursion that I'd missed. The trade unionist from Scotland joined me. He was someone quite well known at home. I'd seen him on television. You meet interesting people on package holidays.

Two tiny boys with curly hair slid from their seats and started jumping and jigging together. A father snatched his little girl from her startled *babushka* to get her on the pony ride just leaving the hotel gate. The fluffy dog stretched under my table was much more interested in sleep than food until the peace parade started to move off and he rushed yapping into line behind the red banners. "No star wars," said the slogans. "Outer space for peace." "Children, the future of the world is yours."

"Aye," said the trade unionist as he surveyed the scene. "So this is it. Reagan's evil empire. The trouble is, nobody listens to you when you get back. D'ye ken, there's some of my mates at work still think they eat their own bairns."

"That little place sure must have been wonderful in its hey-day." It was Herb again, having a last look at Bukhara from the night express to Samarkand.

"Now isn't that just typical. I've said it before, Herb, and I'll say it again. You really are the original male chauvinist."

I hadn't realised there was a Mrs Herb.

"My Herb, now," she turned to me, because I was there, I supposed. "His aesthetic sensibilities were so offended by the television aerials on all these cute, mud-walled houses we passed on the way to the collective farm."

"Just don't forget, Herb," (it was his turn) "when it was all so picturesque, it was the women who carried the burdens. Who was it that walked miles to bring back the pitchers of dirty water on their heads? You wouldn't do that, Herb. Now would you, Herb? I'm speaking to you, Herb."

"No, honey. I mean, yes honey, of course I would."

He wasn't really listening. Nor was I. The tray of tea-glasses in filigree holders had just gone past us to the sleepers. They had a real, charcoal-burning samovar on this train and plump lace-edged pillows on the bunk-beds. On the trains they have music too. I did Leningrad to Moscow once and the Red Arrow slid away to a rather catchy, if somewhat martial tune. It was a night for the slim volume of poetry I'd brought with me and maybe some star-gazing as we continued the Golden Journey eastwards across the Hungry Steppe.

"Away for we are ready to a man.
Our camels sniff the evening and are glad."

James Elroy Flecker, of course. There must be something more appropriate further on.

"But surely we are brave.
Who make the Golden Journey to Samarkand."

I wasn't feeling particularly brave. There wasn't any reason. Just awfully sleepy.

I saw no stars that night either. I didn't even hear the music of the train.

MEMORIES

They met at sunset on the banks of the sacred Ganga, at Shamshaan Ghat. Shamshaan Ghat, the Ghat of Death, where Hindus of all castes, rich and poor, burn their dead, convinced that the deceased will obtain instant salvation from the cycle of birth and rebirth that is the lot of all men. Above them, the giant stone steps mounted majestically from the kingdom of the dead up to the city of the living. Around them spiralled acrid fumes from the rows of corpses laid out on blazing funeral pyres. At their feet lapped the waters of the sacred river, midnight black with the putrid refuse of the city. The last rays of the setting sun illumed with an odd clarity the golden marigolds flecking the river surface and bedecking the bodies of the dead awaiting their final immersion in the Ganga before being set ablaze by the sacred flame gifted by Shiva.

They sat a few feet apart, two women from different worlds. The long straight tresses of one, partially shrouded by the *pallav* of her white sari, contrasted starkly with the cropped curls and dark dress of the other. They watched in silence as a huge shaggy ram passed between them and, straddling a waiting corpse, began to chew mouthfuls from the garlands draping the body. As the keepers of the cremation ground pierced the unburned remains with long poles and hurled them into the river, they exchanged glances. As the dogs, reared from infancy on a diet of human flesh, fought the circling kites for the remains, they began to speak, hesitatingly, each groping for words in the language of the other.

The roads that had led them to Varanasi, to the Ghat of Death, were different. For Sita, the journey had begun in a remote hamlet. In a midnight ceremony she had stumbled, a bleary four-year-old, circumambulating the sacred flame of matrimony behind her eleven-year-old groom, Raja. She remained, however, a child in her parental home, her life unchanged until, mature at thirteen, she was despatched to her husband's house. Even there, her existence did not alter; only the nights were spent with the husband ordained for her by fate. And in a few months her husband left home to seek work in the city. She remained with her mother-in-law, performing her daily chores, waking in the morning before sunrise, lighting the fire for cooking, and fetching water from the well with the other village women before going to work in the fields. At sunset she returned home to perform the evening tasks before sinking onto her straw *charpoy* for a few hours of rest before sunrise and the monotonous grind of another day.

Then one hot, bright afternoon, her husband arrived home from his sweeper's job in the city and announced that he had offered her services as a domestic to his employer. She had packed her few faded saris and well-scrubbed kitchen utensils into a cheap cardboard suitcase, and, trembling with fear and anticipation, had left the security of the village and the home she had known for years for the city in the company of the almost complete stranger she called her husband. In the city, she came to know him. A simple man, an affectionate man, a hard-working man, saving his meagre salary to buy her gifts and brighten the whitewashed walls of their one-roomed apartment. Slowly, by degrees, she came to love him. The only shadow darkening their life was the fact that they had no children.

And then he died. Quite suddenly, on another hot bright afternoon, he came home, ashen-faced. He had clutched his heart, complained of a burning sensation, and, quickly, within a few moments, had died, holding her hand.

She had buried him, with little pomp and less ceremony, in the city. He mattered so little to the world; only a few co-workers attended his last rites. Even his employer was more concerned about losing her services: a sweeper is easier to find than a good domestic. She had remained, therefore, in the city on an augmented salary. What did life hold for her in the village, in any case? She would be a widow, the harbinger of evil, the unlucky one, permitted to wear no colour, permitted to have no colour in her life. She would live out the remainder of her life, unwanted, as the lowest of the low within the shadows of the walls of her husband's home. Here in the city she could at least cloak herself in anonymity among the teeming millions.

She worked and she saved. Gradually she hoarded enough to make the long journey to Varanasi in her thirty-ninth year, to fulfil a promise made to her husband on his funeral pyre: to immerse his ashes in the sacred Ganga and, hopefully, obtain *mukthi* for him.

For Carol, the journey had begun a quarter of a century ago and a continent away, in a small village in the English countryside where she had lived out a tranquil existence as the daughter of the local parson. The son of the village doctor, Mark, her first and only love, had been part of the fabric of her life from her earliest years. Together they had explored the magic realms of childhood and experienced the uncertainties of adolescence. They had married at twenty-one, one summer morning, in a quiet ceremony in the village church. They had filled the small church with roses, and the scent of roses always brought back memories of the ceremony to her: her father fumbling with emotion as he turned the pages of his prayer book, Mark standing tall and straight, the sunlight from the stained glass window spilling a rainbow of colours on his blond head.

She had gone to work as his father's receptionist; he had joined the local solicitor. The even tenor of their days had been punctuated by routine happenings: afternoon tea with scones and wafer-thin cucumber sandwiches, an occasional beer in the local pub, weekend cricket on the village green, evensong on Sundays. No children had arrived and, after a while, they had given up hoping.

And then, quite suddenly, on Christmas eve, in an almost identical fashion to Raja, he had died, clutching his chest and complaining of heartburn. All that winter she had been depressed, haunted by the lyrics of that Beatles' melody, *Eleanor Rigby*. In spring, impulsively, she had taken their little nest-egg, sent telegrams to a friend in India and bought a ticket to Varanasi, to the city of the Ghat of Death.

And now both of them sat together among the living dead, wrapped in memories of their dead. They sat a long while, motionless, watching the brutal simplicity of the ritual of death. Bodies arrived, one after the other, carried by pall-bearers chanting the name of Rama. Distinctions between the living and the dead vanished as all were subjected to the traditional rites. As the flames licked away at the corpses, silk-bedecked, bejewelled forms, drenched in expensive ghee, heaped high with propitious coconuts and laid on pyres of fragrant sandalwood crumbled into the same ashes as cotton-shrouded corpses lashed with rope. The little children, too, were no respecters of mortal differences, as they swarmed out of the serpentine city alleys to scavenge, indiscriminately, the coconuts placed on the dead. As the funeral embers lost their glow, the children came armed with earthenware pots to collect coal to cook their evening meal. The cycle of life played out around the pyres of death.

Night had long since fallen when I went in search of Carol and found them mounting the steps together, an incongruous pair, but touched by the identical sorrows and struggling with similar emotions. I spoke only briefly to Sita as she folded her hands together in the age-old gesture of greeting and farewell. Then, in an awkward motion, she thrust the urn that had contained the ashes of her husband into Carol's hands before slipping away into the darkness.

It was a year later, on the Fourth of July, that I stood with Carol, on the deck of a ferryboat, one of the thousands celebrating at the foot of Lady Liberty. Silently, under the cover of darkness, she slipped her wedding ring, the tangible symbol of bondage to Mark, into the urn before sliding both into the water. At the festival of freedom, she loosened her ties to the dead and turned to me with a smile.

They had met at Shamshaan Ghat, two women from different worlds. They had spanned the light years separating their cultures and derived strength and solace from each other. In identical gestures of renunciation, they had closed the pages of the past and begun life again.

For the Colonel's lady and Judy O'Grady are sisters under the skin . . .

JACQUI STEARN

ROMANCE OF THE NILE

Time flows at a different pace in Egypt. Minutes, hours, days are longer by a ratio of 1:3 – or so we concluded as we sat waiting for Abdullah to return to his felucca. "No problem, we sail at nine," had been his words the previous night. But he'd been gone two hours already, seeking police permissions for us to sail the Nile with him from Aswan to Luxor.

Mark and I had arrived in Aswan two nights previously, transported from the horror of Cairo by sleeper, or rather, encased in an hermetically-sealed time travelling capsule which conveyed us through a panoramic series of tableaux depicting the life of the poor. Outside our German-designed, air-conditioned, muzak-soaked cabin, donkeys turned waterwheels just as they had done in my childhood. Bible pictures, and piles of mud bricks lay baking in the sun. Passing through Kom Ombo, the past and present met in the sight of a truckload of camels, their disembodied heads hovering above the sides, pivoting on their scrawny necks like so many nodding car-shelf dogs.

Piled about our feet on the felucca floor were the groceries we'd bought in the bazaar the night before. Mark and I had been lucky to find a like-minded couple to travel with us and now he was entertaining Miryam and Sjors with his dinner party wit. My thoughts meanwhile drifted back to a memory that was adding new meaning to the phrase "the romance of travel".

Mark and I had decided to travel only a week before we left. We had always been excellent travelling companions, but of late this had failed to permeate our life together. We decided on a holiday to heal the growing rifts and, besides, I wanted a break before starting a new job. The night we flew they held a leaving party for me at work.

Wave after wave of smiling faces came to say goodbye and, as the pile of presents grew, the whole event took on the air of a wedding. What I remembered now was the spark of recognition that had passed between myself and a man whom I'd assumed, by his ease with women, was gay. Sitting in the felucca I realised that the memory was underscoring my experience of Egypt. Here was I embarking on a journey to heal my relationship with one man whilst savouring the possibilities with another. Just as I concluded that it was best to enjoy the present, Abdullah returned, triumphantly waving our passports and pieces of paper. He was three hours late, and from then on the "Egyptian time factor" became a standing joke between the four of us.

Feluccas are traditional wooden sailing boats, and this one belonged to "Capitan" Abdullah. He busied himself around the boat and then, with the ease of a magician's monkey, gathered his gallabiah between his legs and shinned up the mast into the blue void of the African sky. Pulling ropes, he performed the trick of letting loose an expanse of white sail. It instantly filled with wind which had *Bella* straining at her moorings and Abdullah racing to release her. We were off on our first diagonal tack across the mother of rivers.

The tranquillity induced by the quiet glide of sailing back and forth across the Nile has no equal: I understand the origin of "Egyptian time". At times the desert through which the river flowed, seemingly in defiance of nature, was very close; at others it was a shimmering brightness in the distance behind the narrow, fertile strip of crops and palms. The river's immediate banks were fringed with pale-leaved willows, reeds and sedges. Damselflies with slivers of colour for bodies darted back and forth; ibis and herons stood sentinel in the water, the spaces between them territorially measured; pied kingfishers flew the length of the banks with graphic flashes.

Absent from the water's edge were crocodiles, though we found a rotting heap of mummified, toothy grins at the temple of Kom Ombo. Wandering amongst the temple ruins, murder sprang to my mind. It was the classic setting: columns to hide behind; twisting, time-worn steps descending into a cavernous Roman well into which a body could be dragged, cryptic messages on the walls depicting worship of falcon and crocodile gods; and, of course, the cave full of rotting crocodiles. The clusters of Europeans hovering around their tour guides would be perfect for merging into once the foul deed had been done, their cruise ships the setting for discovery of the missing person. And witness to it all? The very vocal temple cat who accompanied me all the while as I imagined the plot, yowling and rubbing my legs.

Murder was often thought of on our vessel too. Mohammed, Abdullah's adolescent assistant, was not the best of deckhands, and his ears were constantly ringing from verbal blows. But the four of us were enjoying each others' company, especially Miryam and I who were growing close. Spending so much time with her and Sjors held a mirror to my own relationship and I found it sorely wanting in an intimacy I yearned for – the rifts were widening, not closing.

After visiting Kom Ombo it was time for the men to shave. Sjors and Mark each had portable razors, but Adbullah's ablution was far more ritualistic. He steered while he soaped, back against the tiller, bare feet braced against the boat's side. Then a few deft strokes with a traditional razor and he'd shaved his chin clean. Smelling Sjor's after-shave – it was impossible not to – he asked to try some. Abdullah grinned as he took the bottle, then smelt the contents and dabbed. Pain screamed from his face the instant the alcohol hit his sore skin and he scooped furiously at the river to wash it off. He passed the bottle back apologetically, shaking his head in puzzlement at Sjors' masochism.

Towards dusk we passed a village where men were gathering on the banks amongst the water buffaloes and donkeys. They hitched up their gallabiahs to wash before going to their evening prayers in the mosque whose minaret punctuated the setting sun. We made for an island and moored for the night as a classic moon of Islam rose to cast its light across our boat. That second night was quiet and still once the muezzin had ceased calling, and remained quiet until the shrill cries of ibis pierced the morning calm. At some point in the night a donkey brayed – a lonely sound.

The next day faced us with the minus side of wind-powered travel – no wind, no travel. Rowing was the only option since we had to reach Luxor that night. After an hour or so of exhausting exercise, sharing the labour of heaving the unwieldly oars, we heard a thrum of engines. It was a barge, and Abdullah suggested we hitch a lift. Standing to wave and catch their attention while yelling at Mohammed to take the oars, he began a swirl of furious activity. As we drew alongside the barge's foredeck, ropes were thrown and attached fore and aft, lashing us close to its dwarfing bulk.

A bell rings from the wheel and we start to gather speed. I'm fasci-nated by the wheel which is huge and being turned hand over hand, foot over foot, by a man straddling its side – he appears to be climbing first up then down. Suddenly he's no longer in view. The fore rope has snapped and we're spinning away from the barge. We shout and wave, urging them to stop and set us completely free. With the felucca weav-ing from side to side the aft rope pulls taut, creaks for an eternity; then it, too, snaps. What a relief. We could have . . . But where is Abdullah? We can't see him anywhere. Convinced he's on the barge and we're drifting alone with Mohammed, panic mounts. Then he shins down the mast.

Two to an oar, we double-row ourselves back to the barge which has slowed to wait. Once again we are lashed together, but this time aft and next to the rudder. Grateful as we are, the journey has changed, the romance obliterated by the mind-numbing throb of engines and stench of diesel. When the wind returns and we're released back into graceful passage down the Nile, the mood of the river has changed too; roads run either side through the green ribbon; cars honk their way across a road bridge spanning its width; sheer walls of concrete

replace the riverbank vegetation; inside the empty boxes of an unfinished apartment block, a horse is tethered, waiting to be washed in
the water. I grow increasingly dismayed at the encroachment of modern Egypt; our Pharaonic voyage is ending.

We left Abdullah and Mohammed just outside Luxor. Later, lying
in a stuffy hotel room above a busy street, my body ached for the rise
and fall of the boat and I wished with all my heart to be back in the
felluca gazing at Abdullah crouched elegantly by the tiller. I remembered the way he pulled his blue gallabiah between his legs, his smart
yellow cap sitting pert on his head of black curls and his deep brown
eyes staring ahead. For the first time in days I remembered a pair of
blue eyes and the look they had given me. I went to sleep dreaming of
them.

JACKI POLANSKI

NAKED AMONGST THE GUZERAT

Juan turned on the generator at 3am. The slap of light catapulted me towards the obligatory shower. By three-thirty Señor Sanchez had arrived to take us on the long journey to Caracas. In air-conditioned blackness we drove past the fan-shaped traveller's palms screening the swimming-pool, past the banana plantation where every day old Eduardo listlessly dribbled the hose over the tall leaves; through the iron gates of the hacienda to cross the wide, lush valley of African stargrass. The herds of Brahman cattle recently delivered from the Llanos plains for fattening stopped grazing momentarily to walk away from the assaulting headlamps. Already their vivid black noses glistened with good health, their silvery hides hanging in draped bands like velvet necklaces swaying gracefully as they munched.

The immaculate Lina placed the bag of tangerines, gathered yesterday from the two big trees by the wash-house, on the seat between us. I decided that in a few minutes I would ask for one.

We shuddered over the cattle-grid onto the common land beside the lake. No grass here, just prickly shrubs and baked mud.

The dry season lasted from January to April, and at night threatening bush-fires lit the surrounding mountains to a fierce red. Don Juan and his herdsmen were skilled in the art of "back-firing". They would light a strip of scrubland below the length of the bush-fire, so that on meeting the two fires exploded and burnt each other out. Sprawled over the track lay the cattle and horses belonging to the Indians. Juan shouted, drumming his palm against the door until the scraggy animals rose up and moved painfully aside. Lina, being used to this procedure, handed around the tangerines. But in the artificial light the look of hopelessness in the eyes of the animals became distressingly accentuated. It was a look I had witnessed constantly amongst human- and animal-kind during my weeks of travel in South America. And

The traditional felucca, the Nile's beast of burden. (*Romance of the Nile*)

not least here in Venezuela, considered the most Americanised of Latin American cultures.

During my first evening Lina graciously asked, "What would you like to see in our country?"

"Angel Falls please."

"But dat is just a long streak of white!"

I shrugged. "Then I shall walk to the mountains to paint."

"No!", wagging forefinger. "You do not go anywhere beyond de wire fencing. De Indians carry machetes and you with your little brush, what do you think you can do? You can get bitten by mapanari out dhere and dat snake-bite is lethal. This is not Kew Gardens, my dear."

I was silenced into appreciating the black bean soup.

So, every morning I accompanied Juan to his offices by the breeding-pens and from there I walked, equipped with drinking-water and reeking in Autan, to look for pictures to paint. I learned not to sit on the track where passing vehicles whipped up dustclouds to smear my brilliant colours. Instead I braved the immensity of space, fighting to keep my brush steady when seven Nelore bulls encircled me, their combined tonnage an awesome counterpoint to the lightness of their tread. They disappeared mysteriously to drown in extensive pastures. I heeded Juan's advice when three barefoot cowboys rode up swiftly, laughing in curiosity, and inclined my head in a formal nod of greeting. These tough Llaneros can write their names and are the fathers of schoolchildren, yet they feel excluded from the modern world. They assemble in their best suits on pay-day to see The Don Juan because he can explain what is written, otherwise the bank clerks may not honour their cheques. For it was he, the fair and courteous *el mister,* who had talked his way out of danger when the military, without notice or explanation, invaded his hacienda. The Don Juan ruled O.K.

I had fallen for the young champion Brahman bull, which always greeted me fluttering endless black eyelashes. I had seen him give sperm for freezing, so I suppose we were on rather intimate terms. "Juan has gone over to the electric ejaculator," Lina announced coquettishly. For reasons of economic progress, Juan had been advised to limit the natural servicing methods of breeding and adapt to artificial insemination. Little realising that I was to witness a ceremony normally forbidden to women, and which few foreigners see, I accepted an invitation to watch my beautiful champ perform. The animal was

Above: A typically decorated dwelling, across the river from Luxor, records a journey to Mecca. (*Romance of the Nile*)

Below: 'My beautiful Champ.' (*Naked Amongst the Guzerat*)

roped and harnessed within a secure pen. Hector's arm then disappeared to the elbow to clear the animal's rectum of faecal residue. Into
it he inserted a metal objected shaped like a toy submarine which was
attached to an instrument-box by two long wires. Champion suffered
this invasion with calm professionalism. Whilst Hector held fast at the
rear, Tiburcio crouched under the penis ready to catch semen in a
scrupulously clean plastic cup. Juan began to administer gently es-
calating doses of electric current. The mounting frequency of his
breathing sucked the bull's haunches inwards and pushed his belly
outwards like a huge pair of bellows at work. After some fifteen
minutes the sugar-pink penis slowly emerged from its tube of muscu-
lar, hairy skin making short contractions. Juan, expert at reading bull
signals, shouted *"Ahora! ahora!"* and in a delirium of spasms Champ
ejaculated his valuable high-progeny-count semen neatly into the cup.
Then, with eyes cast ecstatically heavenward, his body slumped into
the cradling harness. Upon recovery he was patted and praised and
hosed down.

The next bull, a promising Nelore of good growth and scale of
muscling, was a virgin. Not only did he resist the rectal washout but he
fought the toy submarine hard with heaving haunches and persistent
head batterings. It took more than thirty minutes to achieve success,
and then Tiburcio nearly missed his catch. There was no discernible
moment of ecstacy, only tendrils of streaming blood and saliva from
the wounded muzzle. But after the microscope reading Juan pronounced an exceptionally high progeny-count, so young Frisky was
in for a long term of ecstasy-training.

I had formed the habit of swimming an increasing number of
lengths before sundown, and was in the water when Lina called out
flourishing tickets to Angel Falls. To her surprise there was a Tourist
Camp down there, primitive but operational. So we flew in a small jet
southeast from Caracas for several hours. We covered vast patterns of
land, now dazzlingly flat, now sharply undulating, until we landed at
the newly constructed town of Puerto Ordaz on the mighty Orinoco
Delta. The relief pilot stared at us for some moments. Then he
approached with an invitation to share his view from the cockpit.
Within twenty minutes the plane had become a silver-winged
dragonfly skimming over jungle flanked by giant mountains. The presence of these flat-topped Tepuy created one enormous sweeping
canyon. I understood the excitement Jimmy Angel must have felt in
1935 when he discovered the 3,000-foot high falls. Suddenly we were
flying against a great streak of gushing white. The plane had shrunk to
a gnat. Brushing spray, we circled the summit and doubled back.
Now the viewing passengers on the other side could have their shrieking, swooning fainting-fits.

Our thatched cottage at the pretty lakeside village of Canaima pro-

vided unaffected comfort. To escape the bugs we moved the beds well
away from the walls and sprayed everything. Two Indian guides in
scarlet loincloths and feathered headbands took our small party by
canoe along the Rio Carrao. After chasing over rapids and passing
countless waterfalls cascading from the tops of the Auyan-Tepuy we
landed at Orchid Island. There we swam in fresh bronze-coloured
waters and sat on coral sands to eat barbecued chicken and *tequenos*.
Soundlessly from out of the jungle there paddled an old "Dutchman".
He had lived with the Indians for over forty years and would not talk
about himself. He wanted food. Pointing out Vei-Tepuy, the Sun
Mountain, he told us that during May and June the sun rises between
the cleavage of its two breasting peaks. Then tribes, as yet unknown to
the white man, make their sacrifices.

On returning to the hacienda I made my final swim and sprang
dancing from the pool. It was then that I noticed them. The herd of
newly delivered Guzerat had stopped chewing and were gazing at my
swirling nakedness. I could read nothing from their eyes. But the
shape of their high circular horns skirting the bougainvillea hedge
spelled out a long OOOOOOOOOOOOOOOOO!

Like the night, the dawn was now arriving quickly, revealing the
horrors of Los Ranchos, the shanty-towns on the mountainsides
framing Caracas. I handed Juan a card.

"Could Señor Sanchez please take me to this address?"

Lina glanced at me. "What about your trip to Rio?"

"I have to go down to the Guyana, the land of Green Mansions."

"But dhere is nothing to see! Just a lot of tall grass . . ."

TOURIST ATTRACTIONS

It's Britain's playground – a kind of latterday cut-price Cannes, designed for luxury in large numbers. Costa del Sol, mid-eighties – a careful concoction of charms and traditions upgraded into a saleable format for the masses.

Since my last visit to Spain, eighteen years ago, its priorities have changed perceptibly. Flamenco, castanets and threadbare donkeys are now relegated to the second-hand half fantasy of postcards, while fast food, English beer and soccer results phoned direct to Figaro's Wine Bar are today's hard sell.

This visit was an autumn break, planned by the family's women, and I went too. The weather in England had broken, but in two hours' flying time we lost two months of advancing rain, emerging in the Malaga evening to smells of exhaust oil and hot dust, while crickets purred coolly in the airport palms.

The Mediterranean night felt immediately familiar, velvet smooth and wrapped in a composite of old odours – cooking, tobacco and ripe drains. Through scowling passport control, we filed meekly into a dismal hall full of grinding striplights and flies, rescued our rotating luggage and looked around for salvation. It came in the form of the company rep. Her name was Marion – a pale, nervy girl, primly efficient in her starched blue and white, handing out labels, smiles and reassurance like a primary school teacher on a field trip. Hulking porters skulked our baggage away to the waiting coaches under her sharp bilingual command, and soon we were off, already insulated from the country we'd set foot in only twenty minutes before.

My last holiday in Europe was a month in Greece as a student, confronting everything at street level, and I felt slightly cheated as I watched Malaga slip by. Past billboards and under multiple gantries of traffic lights, Marion spoke down the microphone of the city's cultured past, chiefly as Picasso's birthplace. As a backpacking pedestrian I would have found that out at the city museum, or from fellow travellers. Yet this, being a quick and convenient week away, must be a brief, spicy whiff. We were tickled by tasty mouthfuls of fact that had no substance. Nothing was said about Pablo's blue period, or how the light here may have influenced him. My principles were at odds.

We arrived in Torremolinos and travelled its central drag, a long ribbon of hoardings dribbling cascades of coloured light from the mauve sky. It was exactly what I had expected – a kind of up-and-coming amalgam of Las Vegas and the Kings Road, gaudy, shameless and comically misspelt. "Today Specails Onions Omlit – Frendly Englis Grub 500 ptas – Fish Chips at Good Prizes."

Our hotel was by the sea, one of a long row punctuated by palms and dramatic cacti, a series of square blocks washed up by tides of profit and scrubbed clean on the edge of the sand. As we arrived, water was trickling moodily from the mouth of a concrete fish into the hotel pool and the vast creaking succulents by the main door were subtly lit from beneath.

As motley as moths to a late burning lamp, our fellow guests followed no pattern, a command of English being the only thing we all had in common. It was the end of October, and apart from a few family half-termers we represented the season's last squeeze, an ill-assortment of late sun-seekers set on postponing winter. The couple in the room opposite us were elderly, pale, withered and astonished. They had clearly been propped in the plane by a loving daughter who'd sent them off for their first, and possibly last, taste of sun and fun. But they had no stomach for Spain. We saw them tottering along the corridors, wide-eyed and silent, reading off the room numbers like clues in some dismal treasure-hunt. On our second morning, while I was out in the corridor mopping up a spill of orange juice, the man's grey head appeared round his door. We hadn't yet spoken, and now as he peered at me, terrified through his National Health lenses, all he said was "Ants – all over – look." He pushed the door open. His wife was spread-eagled against the wall in terror, and everywhere ants were crawling – over the bed and chairs, up the curtains, in and out of the bathroom. They'd invaded the cold supper the old folk hadn't been able to face the night before. Just then the Spanish maid came along the corridor to save the occasion, bawling unknown arias as she slapped the walls with her feather duster. She took the situation in at a glance, clicked her tongue, made a brief appeal to a suitable saint, then proceeded to wallop her way round the room with little grunts and cries of vengeance and satisfaction. The old couple scuttled away. We saw them later on, sitting in the bar, as pale and straight as chess pieces, sipping Spanish tea and wincing.

Each day unfolded like a page from a glossy mag, a dazed ritual of rising and eating and heading for the paid parcel of beach. Lazing through the vast blue afternoons I read or slept, wrote or listened. Half an hour of quiet would suddenly be shattered by the whine of an electric saw, the lilting wail of the strolling grape-seller, or a row erupting over a Spanish lunch somewhere on an unseen balcony. A barrage of curses and cutlery bounced off the opposite wall in a brief volley of venom, then lapsed. Showers of sparrows rose and resettled, and the beach of bodies turned, yawned and abandoned itself to a further delirium of sun.

In the evening there was shopping to be done, and this job fell to me. Out from the traffic of children, I strolled solitarily into the steadily declining day, along the tree-lined Calle de la Luna, past its shuttered bars and scattering cats. It was a cool shadowy street with a pavement of patterned ceramic squares, sheltered by withered walnut trees and heaped clusters of a kind of blue-flowered bindweed that trailed loose knotted runners down the whitewashed walls.

The shops were on the top road, the main Malaga to Cadiz through-way, a bustling torrent of cosy malls in which I found a small family supermarket full of relabelled imports and large plastic drums of drinking water piped fresh from the hills. The son spoke to me in English and I addressed him in Spanish, everything was slickly wrapped in germ-free foil, and from somewhere on a hidden tape loop, like a ritual reminder, Chris Rea sang *On The Beach*.

This new cultural duality was what struck me most about Spain as I saw it now. We took a day-trip down the coast to Gibraltar, and only then became aware of the huge scale of its adaptation to Britain. Apart from the larger centres like Fuengirola and Marbella the open coun-tryside of scrub, scrawny goats and parched vines is all being sys-tematically bulldozed and built on. Little estates of white Spanish fan-tasy are creating new and nameless suburbias enclosed by flashcard hoardings in broken English advertising the obvious. There's no con-necting plan or scheme. Some of the cheaper flats are plain prisons, the smaller houses self-consciously immaculate, prettily perched in glades of imported forest, sprouting banks of countrified colour from the well-watered dust; a re-creation of Peacehaven with additional patios and palms.

It's the sheer scale and newness of it that unnerves me. Apart from a handful of wrecked hovels in the hills, there's no building over twenty years old the length of that sun-parched shore. Nothing of Spain exists there, and having no history it has no balance. Instead it's a culture under construction, divided sharply into consumers and consumed; an explosive burgeoning of beaches, bank accounts and two half-languages, clipped into rifle-shot phrases for ease of understanding – "Molly Malone's Bar – English Irish Sangria."

So I had learned little of myself or of Spain on this holiday, except perhaps a reflected view of the image it has of me; one of a tribe of beer-swilling, chip-chewing oblivion-seekers.

Yet for all that, there were moments of extreme magic for which I would return. On the morning of my birthday I rose early and went down to the beach with a camera. There I watched the sun rising, billowing up from the horizon at the speed of an airborne bubble, sending sharp angles of blood-red reflection over the wrinkled sea. A jet, climbing from distant Malaga, crawled across the crimson sky like a thunderbug. These, along with other scents and sensations, form the cargo of memories I'll tie up and take home, all of them tenuous and intangible, probably to be unlocked at some later time by the laconic guitar and lost voice of Chris Rea singing *On The Beach* beneath a bank of English cloud.

TOM MEINHARD

"In the Blue Ridge Mountains of Virginia on the Trail of the Lonesome Pine . . ."

The Blue Ridge Mountains are the first ridge of the Appalachians as you cross the coastal plains from the Atlantic and step up off the Piedmont plateau. Famed in the Laurel and Hardy theme song, they rise fold on rounded fold of thick hardwood forest, to some 6,000 feet.

Three hours' drive from the steaming sauna which is Washington in the summer, and 3,800 feet up in the clear air of the Blue Ridge Mountains, lies the Wintergreen Mountain Resort. Perched a few miles west of Thomas Jefferson's Monticello and the University of Virginia which he founded, the resort is stamped by a distinctive feature. The facilities are owned and controlled by the property owners, who have bought sites and built second homes within the Wintergreen area. The owners underwrite a management company for the resort, securing it against insensitive over-development and downmarket pressures with a degree of success which has made them keenly studied and imitated by leisure resorts elsewhere.

Wintergreen covers 11,000 acres of mountain forest, with recreation facilities of general range and quality. A par-70 golf course has been cut out of the forest and winds for 6,500 yards across blue grass fairways and watered greens, with sudden mountain vistas fifty miles across the Great Valley to the Alleghenies. There are sixteen tennis courts, outdoor and indoor swimming, pony trails and lakes for swimming and canoeing in the valley below. There are twenty miles of marked tracks through the forests, and guided nature trails to study plants, trees, fungi, wildlife, geology. Ten ski slopes, including 1,000-foot vertical falls and snow-making equipment, provide for a three-month ski season, with lifts and floodlit skiing.

And yet, all this is lost within the vastness of the mountains and the forests. Nature overwhelms man. Rocks formed 1,100 million years

ago fold into mountain ridge lines, valleys and rock faces, where plant
and animal life have found their niches. Variations in slope direction,
altitude and moisture give shelter to different forms of wildlife.
Natural gardens have established themselves, in different microsites,
with different plants. Springs rise, streams are fed, waters tumble
down mountainsides, over rock slides, through trout pools. Deep
gorges are cut. Shamokin gorge (a Monocan Indian word meaning
"land were the antlers are plenty") at Wintergreen drops almost 3,000
feet from the top of the rocky slide down into the creek bed.

The main trees I see are shagbark hickory, red oak, white ash, yellow birch. Also chestnut oak, with their gnarled twisted trunks, table
mountain pine and huge Canadian hemlock up to six feet in diameter.
These form the leaf canopy overhead, and insulate the forest floor
from the hot sun. By late September the hickory leaves have turned
bright yellow, and Virginia creepers add blazes of vivid red. Very
soon now the forest will turn, and the trees take on their autumn colours. At head height, rhododendron, azalea and mountain laurel
abound, promising brilliant colour in early summer. American
chestnut, reduced by a disastrous blight at the beginning of the century, struggles cyclically back to shrub height before disease cuts it
down to the roots again. Underfoot meanwhile, my scant botany cannot keep pace with the profusion of wild flowers and fungi. On one
short trail I count twenty-one different plants in bloom. Yellow lady
slipper is in flower. So too is ginseng, with its red berry fruit, a protected plant whose dried root fetches $300 a pound for export to the
Far East. There are oxeye daisies, yarrow and crown vetch; numerous
varieties of fern; wood nettle and its antidote, jewel weed; wild vine,
wild orchids and lilies.

I walk in the forest all day without seeing or hearing a soul. Now the
going is flat; now I am scrambling over large rocks, across streams, up
steep slopes. The forest is wide awake and I hear the continual muted
plop of falling acorns, the piping squeaks of the chipmunks, the
whistling of jays, the raucous bark of the slope-soaring ravens. Sound
carries in the mountains. Now and again a heavier thud denotes the
falling of dead wood, perhaps close by, perhaps way over on the opposite slope – the forest sheds twenty-five tons an acre every year. When I
sit quite still, for several minutes, the wood mice emerge to explore
me. The chipmunks, jaw pouches grotesquely distended with freshly
garnered acorns, scamper stiff-legged and tail erect to where I watch;
but they never look me in the eye. Water-thrush sit in the ninebark by
my head. Bear, deer, bobcat and the emblematic wild turkey, are lurk-
ing in these forests unseen.

Without the trail–blazes painted on the trees I would soon be lost.
Outside the marked track I am following, the forest is trackless. It is as
Roman and medieval Europe must have been, a place of danger,

where bandits could lurk, where Arminius could ambush Varus and slaughter three legions, where Robin Hood could hold the Normans at bay. Safe in the twentieth century, I note that the forest is impenetrable, that I can discern virtually nothing beyond about a hundred yards, and I understand how ancient forests could dominate the imagination, breeding fear and mystery, fairy tales and folk myths, dragons and witches.

For some hours I follow the Appalachian Trail. This footpath runs for 2,000 miles from Georgia up to Maine, and as it passes through Wintergreen it follows the high mountainside through the trees, emerging now and again at spectacular rocky escarpments. On one of these I sit for an hour in the hot sun, high out on a projecting rock, and look down across the rolling forest carpet and out to the Shenandoah valley below me. On the facing slope I see large white scree slides of antietam quartzite, which the Indians sought out for its special hardness and used for their arrow heads, scalping knives and tools. Hawks and ravens circle below me, lazing on thermals, hiding in haze and mist banks, waiting to thunderbolt their prey. I note that clichés, even while being clichés, can be true, that the endless treetops *are* a carpet, that the forest *does* shimmer with energy, that the mountains *do* slumber, that the heat *is* drowsy, that this is a Big Country.

After nightfall I sit in my luxury "condo" and sip a Virginia riesling. Suddenly the peace is ambushed by rushing volleys of rain arrowing down. Windlessly, huge drops plunge on to the trees and the leaves, overflow the gutters, splash on to the balcony and roll on down the forest slope. After an hour, just as suddenly, the storm stops, but it continues to echo, dripping from leaf to leaf, from leaf to ground, from eaves to gutter, each note different. The spring peepers have taken over, small green tree frogs emitting a ceaseless and unvarying shrill note like a million small whistling alarms in the liquid night. Framed in the open window of foliage above my head, stars are undraped, and I discern part of the Great Bear, Cassiopeia, the Pole Star, and a brilliant Jupiter loudly proclaiming his mythic role as king of heaven.

Nineteen-eighty-seven is the bicentenary of the American constitution – that nimble document crafted by wealthy slave-owners and disciples of Hobbes, as they convened through the summer of 1787 at Constitution House in old Philadelphia. This was while King George still ruled, and the colonists were anything but victorious. What better pretext – if pretext were needed – to visit the founding fathers at Monticello, at Ash Lawn, in Philadelphia, in Washington, and (mindful that the first president took all of four days to travel from his Mount Vernon home and take up office in New York) to temper unalloyed history with a diversion into nature, by paying a visit to Wintergreen.

BRIAN ATHERTON

EMERALD IMPRESSIONS

Priests, peat and new bungalows, brightly painted like seaside villas, surrounded by rock-studded fields with everything dampened by mist, outlines softened, merging into clinging folds of clouds. "Guinness is good for you." The Abbey Theatre. Signposts to Howth. Joyce and Donleavy. First impressions – my mind clicking like a camera, focused on clichés.

"Dublin, the Fair City." A coach driver drivels on as we drive alongside the Liffey, channelled out to sea, green seaweed slime on the blackened stone parapets. The channel opens out to quays where two ships are docked and beyond lie shades of grey, some dark, some light, growing lighter towards the horizon.

A lady on her way home to Galway says to me: "So it's Kerry you're going to. You'd better wrap youself up warm. Always cold it is. And raining."

What about the Gulf Stream then? She's travelling with a pensioner from England, smart M&S tweed jacket and brown shoes as polished as brass.

"Irish Army I was in the thirties. Bit of a boxer. Lightweight, you know."

"And so was my brother, a lightweight," she chips in.

Though trying desperately to remember the name he can't.

"Dublin's changed out of all recognition," he concludes, becoming a little sad, misty-eyed.

"Well, it would have done after all these years." She sighs, looking away and casting a lingering gaze over the grey skyline.

Curtains of rain, driven by south-westerly squalls, plaster the carriage windows as they streak across the countryside. Standing in a playground full of schoolboys, a priest turns and stares at the train waiting in a station; a drab black and orange train. It seems half the passengers are either priests or nuns. Another priest, German I think, zips open a travelling Bible and glances at it surreptitiously until his companion returns to her seat. With bright red trousers and a black raincoat, she looks very mid-European, very chic, but out of place. Her face is photogenic, jaw bones angular, and the guard is excessively polite to her. But I'm not sure about the priest somehow.

Coming down from Carrauntoohil, lonely but magnificent, Ireland's highest mountain, I hitch a ride with a Cork couple, though the woman is in fact French.

"Australian are you?" they ask, confused perhaps by a weather tan. "We don't meet many English, certainly not hitching." In a pub drinking Guinness we talk about Gaelic football. Inevitably conversation comes round to unemployment, "eighteen per cent and rising" despite constant emigration to Britain and America; spoken of as a workman's paradise, free of red tape, it's streets still paved with gold.

"Don't think me naive," I query, "but there are such things as work permits. And how would you get started?"

He gives me a knowing smile. "There's a shortage of skilled tradesmen, builders like myself, and I've got friends there earning $1,000 a week, no questions asked. Besides, most of the police are Irish."

In Dingle buildings are painted eye-catching colours, brightening up rows of dreary terrace houses; blues and pinks clashing with greens and yellows in gaudy splendour. When the sun shines all the Guinness signs sparkle, black and creamy up the main street. Walking into the bus office, a tiny shop full of parcels behind dust-encrusted windows, I find two men sipping the nectar at a bar. For a moment I wonder if I'm in the right place. "Oh yes, the bus leaves at noon just across the street."

Clean and green, swept bare by salt-stung winds, the Dingle Peninsula juts thirty miles out into the Atlantic, ending with the Blasket Islands, next parish America. Along the northern coast dizzy cliffs tumble into foaming seas. Spray mists over fields cropped close by Kerry cows grazing wide-bellied and docile, with fuchsia blooming in the hedgerows. Dogs and cats, half asleep, laze in a farmyard, the dogs not bothering to chase or bark, being engrossed in contemplating the muck-covered yard, heads on paws. An old man, jacket off in the heat, digs potatoes in a walled garden hard by the ocean. Sunlight sparkles out to islands floating far-off and hazy.

There are ruins everywhere, ancient and modern: Ogham, standing, stones inscribed in a primitive form of morse, commemorating pagan ancestors, some later defaced by Christianisers; beehive huts being used to keep hens; bits of castles blasted down by the English; and remains of the *Ryan's Daughter* filmsets, cobbled roads leading mysteriously into bogs and over cliffs. Without much explanation a guidebook states that Daire Donn, King of the World, was killed in the latter stages of the battle of Ventry. Who was this King of the World? Refugees, outcasts, pilgrims and holymen, shipwrecked sailors of the Spanish Armada – by accident or design people were drawn to this area, living a spartan existence, the hardiest on remote pinnacles of rock cut off from the mainland by treacherous stretches of water.

A couple, both in new Aran sweaters, walk out of a small hotel in Dingle. From inside comes the sound of an Irish folk song playing on the radio. While loading up their car, the husband sings along in a loud voice. "Why don't you put that case in the trunk, honey?" There are plenty of American and Australian tourists about, all of whom think Ireland is wonderful.

"I've been here four months already," an Australian girl tells me in a pub. She's not going anywhere else. A group of locals, fishermen and farmers, are clustered round the bar, flat caps on and creamy pints in hands, chatting together in lyrical whispers and shooting glances at us every now and again.

"I love hearing them talk. It's so poetic, Gaelic. I wish I knew what they're saying."

She probably wouldn't.

"There's really no such language as Gaelic," I inform her. "The Irish for Irish is Gaelic if you follow me." But she just looks perplexed.

Only men are drinking at the bar, mostly old or middle-aged, while their women are at home and their children have gone away to look for work. In the Dingle area alone there have been four suicides in a month; young people driven to it by hopelessness and despair – another world behind the smiles.

At the Oratory of Gallurus, an early Christian stone monument shaped like an upside-down curragh and still in perfect condition, an old man calls me over; a small wiry farmer, unshaven, clothes stained; the three buttons of his combinations showing at the neck. There are badges on his jacket lapels; one I LUV N.Y., another *RELAX*. At his feet basking in the sun are two mongrels. One of them raises its head, an ear pricked, staring at me crossed-eyed. The matter of my nationality is sorted out. Being English it seems I'm in favour, the party of Aussies who have just left not having been too forthcoming with tips. Pointing with a pitchfork and sometimes grabbing my hand, he rattles on hardly pausing for breath; an almost indecipherable mixture of Irish and dialect English, something about a field dispute and a certain Mrs Baker, a local witch he once saw flying. As he talks, a brown dribble runs from the corner of his mouth down his chin, which he wipes with the back of a peat-stained hand. He guides me across adjoining fields, claiming this stone is a burial site, another, hidden under nettles, a sacred monument. The whole performance costs only 25p.

Two farmers drinking tea in a farmhouse look up surprised as I stroll past late in the afternoon. Following the Saints Road I climb Mt. Brandon (3,127ft), spiritual home to St. Brendan. Far below me the peninsula rolls away to the sea, a ripple of emerald green dotted with farmhouses, the stone walls fine as pencil lines. Clouds race overhead covering the summit. Near the top they suddenly break, revealing an iron cross.

It's late now. Silhouettes of headlands and islands float on an orange sea. The moon rises, so I stay high watching the sun set and finally camp well after dark.

An old peat cutter, driving sheep and leading a nag pulling a high-sided cart like something from the Hebrew Slaves, plods up a track on the other side of the mountain. "Hello there," he says, taking a fag end from his mouth. Checking he's not seeing things he turns and takes another look: a man coming down from the mountain at ten in the morning!

Cottages and farmhouses, bright with flowers, cats and dogs. An old lady going to the shop, a black shawl wrapped over her head, clutched tight at the neck by a bony hand. Another old man, in usual dark suit and cap, only smarter this time.

"So you've been up The Mountain have you," he says, reverence in his voice but a twinkle in his Irish eyes.

CLIFFORD BURDEN

ADAM'S PEAK AND
NEWTON'S UNDERPANTS

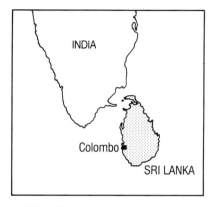

For five years it had been the land of make-believe and Duran Duran videos. Now in five hours it would be reality.

But in transit at Dubai I learned that even on Sri Lanka – The Resplendent Land – fantasy and reality might not match. A Sinhalese greengrocer from Bedford and his teacher niece sowed the first seeds of doubt.

Him: "Malaria's bad up north this year."

Her: "Ignore people who say they're teachers and boy scout leaders and ask for money . . . they're conmen."

Back to uncle: "Don't swim in Colombo's lakes. They're full of crocodiles."

Her: "And never leave valuables on the beach – thieves are everywhere."

What were they saying? I felt as I had when a sadistic babysitter said Father Christmas wasn't real – cheated of something wonderful.

Thoughts of thieves, crocodiles and malaria were cast aside by pondering the treats I had in store . . . sun, a thousand miles of beach to choose from, the holy mountain of Adam's Peak, maybe seeing reclusive millionaire writer Arthur C. Clarke.

Thirty minutes by bus and eighteen miles south of Sri Lanka's Bandaranaike airport is Colombo 1, the capital's business centre. From here I went by thuk-thuk to Colombo 4 in search of rooms.

Thuk-thuk is the onomatopoeic name for the brightly-coloured three-wheeled taxis that are Colombo's cheapest, nimblest and, for the uninitiated, most terrifying form of public transport. My driver pointed to one smashed and abandoned by the roadside. "No problem," he said, dismissing it with a wave.

Accommodation was also no problem. A room with double bed, ceiling fan (essential with the humidity), mosquito coil and Gideons Bible cost £3 a night.

Less happy was the state of Colombo 4's beach. Wooden huts were built in the shade of ragged palms on filthy sand. Most had gaunt, wasted-looking occupants. One offered his wife for the night in exchange for heroin.

Only the sight of a Sri Lankan sunset overshadowed the sordid encounter. The fiery spectacle is swift, as the island is just 340 miles from the equator. As the sun cooled itself in the Indian Ocean, I was joined by a bare-chested man who introduced himself as a history teacher called Ranjid. He grimaced when I confessed I knew nothing of his country's history.

"Few do," he said glumly, and set about correcting this ignorance. He said the island had 2,500 years of written history alone, and that materials and animals in King Solomon's famous temple – the gold, silver, ivory, apes and peacocks – came from Sri Lanka.

He also spoke passionately about the island's most revered monarch, Sri Sanghabodhi Raja, who ruled in 252AD. A price was put on his head after he renounced his sovereignty for religious reasons. And in the ultimate act of self-sacrifice he severed his own head so that a beggar could claim the reward.

Ranjid said: "We have troubles today but only a few – always the few – want violence. Sri Lanka is a beautiful and peaceful place."

My days in Colombo were anything but peaceful and beautiful. There were maniacal motorists, persistent peddlars and stultifying heat and humidity. Day temperatures averaged ninety degrees. My skin burned in the sun, even through cloud.

A chance for escape came through a beach meeting with a self-proclaimed doctor and teacher – yes, another teacher! – calling himself Newton. He said he liked helping tourists – so, charmed but wary, I went with him to Colombo's archaeological museum and tourist information centre. I mentioned Adam's Peak, whereat Newton promptly invited me there on a pilgrimage with his family.

Honoured, but more wary, I asked how I could repay him.

"Give me a pair of your underpants," he said. "St Michael's Marks and Spencer underpants. They don't make them like that here." We shook hands on the deal.

Adam's Peak is thirty miles south of the famous tea region of Kandy in Sri Lanka's central mountainous region. It is a naturalist's paradise, with a wealth of trees, vegetation and wildlife. Thousands of pilgrims climb what must be the longest stairway in the world to pray in the temple at its summit.

Enshrined in the temple is a holy footprint. Orthodox Buddhists believe it belongs to Gautama Buddha, left in memory of his third and

Above left: Ogham stone on the Dingle Peninsular.
Above right: Adding a local touch to a building in Dingle.
Below: Great Blasket Island – 'next parish America'. (*Emerald Impressions*)

Unawatuna Bay in Sri Lanka.
ABOVE: Fishermen perched on poles keep an all-night vigil.
BELOW: Bed in a beach hut for £2 a night.
(*Adam's Peak and Newton's Underpants*)

final visit to Sri Lanka. Mohammedans believe it belongs to Adam and suggests Sri Lanka was the elysium given to Adam and Eve after being exiled from Eden.

If so, they must have been fit.

Slippery, steep terrain, hordes of mosquitoes, clammy heat and warm torrential rain combined to make me wonder what had happened to my fantasy of three weeks in paradise.

Bed for the first night was a pillow and concrete floor at one of three rest camps strung up the mountain. A violent thunderstorm woke me to the sight of a leech feeding on my bloodied right leg. "This part of the mountain is famous for leeches," explained Newton cheerfully, woken by yells. "Don't worry, it will soon drop off."

Leg or leech, I wondered?

But I never moaned aloud. Newton's mother-in-law was why. She was seventy-four, overweight, climbed slowly, often in pain – always without complaint. Newton said it was her first pilgrimage. "She draws strength from the mountain," he said. "Nothing will stop her reaching the top."

We climbed the final stages at night, singing to keep up our spirits, our way lit by sodium lamps buzzing with moths and mosquitoes. At the summit we waited with more than 250 pilgrims and tourists for sunrise. A plump American marvelled at how long it had taken us. "Jeez, we made it in six hours!" he bragged. Later I learned most tourists use a route that let them drive two-thirds of the way, thus criminally ignorant of the original 900-year-old path we had trod.

Buddhists believe the sun bows its respects to the mountain when it first rises, but although confirmation of this was stopped by an untimely rash of clouds, sunrise was breathtaking. The mountain's shadow was hurled miles westwards in a perfect triangle on crowds below us. *"Sabu!"* (holy) the pilgrims chanted.

I asked about the holy footprint. "Covered to stop vandalism," said Newton.

The climb was memorable for many reasons – the most painful being my legs seizing up for three days back in Colombo. Swimming eased the pain but the sea was getting rough. Colombo and the west coast are at their best from August to March. At other times the east coast is better. Because Sri Lanka's central mountains produce two climates in a country smaller than Ireland, no time is a bad time to visit, and anywhere can be reached within a day's drive.

Tattooed with mosquito bites and sunburn – mementoes from Adam's Peak – I fled the chaotic chaos of Colombo for the tranquillity of the south coast. I left after a disastrous day when, having limped to the beach for a swim, I almost drowned in rough seas, lost my Sony Walkman to a monster wave and was crowned with a present dropped by an unsympathetic seagull.

I escaped by bus to Unawatuna Bay and at last found paradise! The name means "There It Fell Down", from a story in the epic Sanskrit poem *The Ramayana,* of an ancient monkey general sent to an Indian mountain to find a magic herb. The general found the mountain but not the herb, so had to carry the entire mountain back to Sri Lanka, carelessly dropping a piece in the bay.

I saw no mountain, but miles of sandy, palm-fringed beach. The sand was stroked by waves tamed by colourful coral reefs, beyond which seals and turtles bobbed and waved. By day the beach was deserted. At night fishermen emerged to perch on poles at sea and wait for the rising moon to tempt fish to the surface for food. Bed in a wooden shack cost £2 a night.

Having found paradise I was tempted to stay. But back in Colombo I had one aim to achieve – visiting reclusive writer/scientist/lecturer and diver Arthur C. Clarke.

If finding his address was a surprise, then discovering the man at home was a shock great enough to sweep from mind all the questions I'd half-heartedly prepared.

We shook hands in a sunroom filled with tropical plants, where the writer autographed one of his books, said I was crazy to stay in Colombo a week and seemed impressed by my visit to Adam's Peak.

"Went there myself once," he said. "Put my legs out of action for three days."

"Me too!" I almost shouted in surprise at this unexpected shared experience.

"A memorable place," he said.

I agreed.

ROY MANLEY

JET LAG

Gatwick-Auckland-Wellington in one go must be as far as you can travel sensibly by air. About 12,500 miles, it must be a jet-lagger's paradise. Over twenty-five hours in the air, with stops in Los Angeles and Tahiti and a transfer in Auckland. Although some, be it admitted, say flying eastwards is worse.

It didn't start well, with ten hours' delay in Gatwick. But at least, as it is the 29th of June, I see the final of the World Cup – and of *Mastermind*. The former watched by two hundred and the latter by twenty in the pub's lounge. Gatwick Village (did my friend who designed the whole place really succumb to such folksiness?) works. It is inhabited by locals as well as passengers – beer and hamburgers and thinking that we, too, might be on our way to Majorca. There is a slightly desperate Sunday night party atmosphere to it all.

In the departure lounge two drunk men fight: one threatening, brown and blond in overalls; the other, half his size, backing away. The police appear and separate them. I hope they're not travelling on the same plane or sharing the same resort. The calls for Spain flicker down the departure board.

Ten hours late, we embark. I'm told that the delay can be traced back to Singapore two days earlier when the crew demanded more stopover time. I have a vision of Gatwick-Auckland flights henceforth always being ten hours late. "Due to an unavoidable delay in Singapore back in the middle-eighties."

I experience three cabin crews, Kiwis to a man and woman, none now remembered, except one steward who flew the last leg and did not smile. They are all helpful and interested, and generous to a fault with Air New Zealand's drink.

The character of the flight changes with the passengers and the stopovers. Ten-and-a-half hours to Los Angeles, families with kids going to Disneyworld. One family spreads over the two seats beside me and the three seats in front. The mother is slim and young for her age and doesn't withdraw when, by accident, our arms touch. They're emigrating to New Zealand and want to give the three kids a last treat. So they'll stay in a Howard Johnson hotel in Los Angeles for two (rapidly becoming one) nights. The father wears a beard and has his working tools with him. They've never been beyond Spain before; I admire the bravery of this leap into the dark.

Los Angeles. An antiseptic transit lounge. Plate glass windows overlook a baggage hall with three vast Stars and Stripes. It's 6.30am local time on Monday. Our ground hostess, beside what she calls a podium, blond, morning fresh, invites us to see her if we have any problems. I ask her for change for the telephone and her eyes glaze over. The coffee bar, racketty and splattered with coloured bulbs, out of place here, opens at seven. A Yorkshire businessman smacks his lips at the weak, tasteless, if unlimited, coffee. I get my coins.

The telephone box spits them back at me, a recorded voice demanding I insert the right amount, which I had. The operator rescues me. They've had a lot of trouble like that with the phones at the airport. Now I'm talking to my ex-brother-in-law: "I'm at Los Angeles airport," I say. "Sorry," he replies.

It's breakfast time on the plane. Indeed, flying west is flying into a series of breakfast times. It's over eight hours to Tahiti. The families gone, the seats fill up with young travellers. Across the aisle from me a group of four I can't begin to place: not friends but colleagues, too young to be businessmen or civil servants. Obviously British, even to the travel-stained checked shirts. Two days later I see their photographs in a New Zealand paper: the Jesus College University Challenge Team. That's why, I think, they were reading so much.

A chaos of Frenchmen, dark chinned and exuberant have joined the plane. They drink whisky, beer and wine for breakfast, filling the aisles. One carries cognac which he takes from the bottle and offers around. Another begins to make advances to a plump blond New Zealand woman sitting behind me. She has sunk two or three glasses of whisky and is beginning to go. Soon she's as pale as a sheet and rushing for the lavatory. He persists as she tries to go to sleep, bringing her a huge pink cuddly bear which he has conjured from nowhere. Her "Fuck offs", surely international, don't work. I use my French to save her from further persecution.

The cocktail party continues, spasmodically. For an hour or two *The Young Sherlock Holmes* transports us into Victorian London. Some incalculable time ago, but on this very plane, I had been in Chicago with Goldie Hawn.

Later, on the eight-hour flight from Los Angeles to Tahiti, the New Zealand blond is beginning to sober.

"I hate Frenchmen," she tells me through the seat. "I don't like their politics. What's his name . . . their president?"

"Mitterand," I reply.

"That's the fucker!"

"Don't worry," I say. "They'll be off in Tahiti."

"But so shall I!"

They are not off in Tahiti. They join me in the transit lounge. A tricolor flies in front of the airport building. The French don't give away colonies unless they have to.

There's that evocative tropical smell, musky, sweet, peppery; and an air of festivity, like a smaller, neater, cleaner Malaga. I wonder where the Gatwick protagonists are now. Well in to the second day of their holidays, separated, one hopes, by a stretch of Mediterranean sea or beach. I buy a Sprite for 1½ US dollars from a fat Tahitian woman at the bar. The thin one charges 3 US dollars.

The last lap, to Auckland, only five-and-a-half hours, just 2,541 miles. Child's play. I think we have lunch, or it could be dinner. It wasn't yet another breakfast. I sleep for two hours; that's six hours in all. The Frenchmen are becoming serious. As we approach Auckland they don jackets with emblems. They are teams of mechanics flown out to service the cars in the New Zealand Rally. I feel fine but recognise frayed nerves when the immigration officer asks for my plane tickets, now pocketed in my case. He deals with my irritation with gentle courtesy.

I obey instructions, queue tidily at the ticket desk at the international airport, am told that they've got me on to the next flight from the domestic airport to Wellington, wait patiently for a tawdry bus, queue tidily again at the check-in for my Wellington flight and am told that my ticket should have been altered and that I can't check in. Could I go to the ticket desk? Here in front of me is a man trying to catch a flight in ten minutes. I still have a quarter of an hour. The clerk appears to be dealing with a woman booking a space flight.

I put my bags in a trolley and dash for the departure gate. No boarding card, no entry. I return to the ticket desk and demand to see the manager. He is on the telephone. The plane leaves in three minutes. He appears. I stay calm and say that I am going to be a real problem to him if I remain in the airport. And then I am dashing again, boarding card in hand to the plane.

I'm in Wellington some forty-four hours after I left home, and with friends. We drink and talk family. It's about midnight New Zealand time on the 1st of July.

I wake up early the next morning. I think of the rules and advice given me by solicitous friends about long distance travel, all of which I ignored. I have done what my body told me to do at the time. I feel great.

DAVID ROSE

LAST DAYS

The Empire still lives. Though Kipling might not recognise Belize International Airport with its Rapier missile batteries, the city would look familiar enough. It stands – just – crumbling into the clear blue waters of the Carribean, the some-time capital of a former British colony.

Generations of schoolchildren knew this little bit of pink in Central America as British Honduras, the name given it nearly 125 years ago, and changed only in recent years to Belize. Since independence in 1981 little else has altered. There still exists the territorial dispute with Guatemala, the roots of which go back to the seventeenth century. Britain even now protects and defends its former colonies against the heirs of the Spanish Empire.

Most of Belize City could be classed as antique, the architecture ranging from Victorian gothick to Wild West frontier. Even the most casual visitor is struck by the belief that it will not long survive. Yet it won't be Club Med, or the package tour trade, which will eventually destroy Belize City. Continuing neglect and another poorly-aimed hurricane will be enough.

The people, too, are a mixture of Belize's many conquerors and settlers. Mayas, Mestizos, Spanish, Creoles, Garinagu, Chinese, East Indians, Lebanese and the British have all left their mark on the 155,000-strong population – a good third of whom are crammed into Belize City.

As soon as you arrive in Belize, someone will proudly boast that nobody starves here. True, there is little evidence of undernourished youngsters or the grinding poverty found in other central American cities; and for once the tourist literature could fairly say "the people are warm-hearted and friendly". Yet the outsider's overwhelming first impression is of a people and a country in terminal decline.

As our Land Rover pulled up outside the city's covered fish market, the smell of decay hung in the air. According to the Hollywood dream factory, places like Belize City should have the scent of tropical orchids or ripe fruit. Instead, up-ended turtles and sharks rotted slowly in the wet heat.

In a very short time I learned from one of the resident British military officers that the sort of Caribbean paradise I had conjured up rarely
existed outside the mind or a film set. And if it did, he pointed out, the
Americans would already have moved in.

There are many good reasons for the well-heeled tourist – and most
everyone here who could be so described is American – to visit Belize.
Two of the best are the barrier reef and desert island cays, the most
popular of which is San Pedro, close to the Mexican border in the
north. This is an area also popular with British soldiers resting from
patrolling the jungle interior or protecting the airfield, so the beach
often has an air of the Spanish Costas about it.

The elderly American couple didn't seem to mind at all that their
hitherto secluded spot on the beach was now under occupation by the
British military. Instead they passed around thickly-cut slices of deer
sausage and accepted in return a few mouthfuls of fizzy drink. The in-
trusion was a minor inconvenience which could be accepted with
good grace. After all, as one of them pointed out, these boys were
keeping a little bit of Uncle Sam's backyard fit for two rich old Texans
to see out the remainder of their days, without the American taxpayer
having to fork out a cent.

It seemed just a bit too cynical. "Come here every year. For the
jaguar shooting. Most peaceful place on earth." The old man smiled at
the prospect of another twenty years bagging big cats. Apparently he
had also shot the deer which provided the filling for our sandwiches.

The Belize International Hotel was now in some demand, as a film
crew had taken over the two first-class hotels in the city. Hanging
around the foyer, I listened to the radio which the two receptionists
always kept switched on. They never listened to it, preferring instead
to gossip in the peculiar Creole *patois*. By the end of my stay I was convinced that neither could understand English, and both just politely
smiled in response to any question or request. Somehow we muddled
through, and with more laughter and good humour than I've ever experienced in a Western hotel.

The morning news kicked off with the biggest story of the day.
After the pop music died away, a woman announcer began in a deep
sombre voice: "The British Air Chief Marshal, Sir Peter Harding,
KCB FRAeS CBIM RAF will visit the High Commissioner, Dame
Minita Elmira Gordon, GCMG GCVO, in Belmopan later today. Sir
Peter is on an inspection visit of the Royal Air Force. He arrived yesterday." Each set of initials after the names was perfectly spelt out. It
took longer that way, and left less of a hole to fill in the rest of the
broadcast.

Not much was happening right then in this tropical outpost of
Britain's lost empire. Harrison Ford was filming *Mosquito Coast* some-

where in the interior; Sir Peter was meeting Dame Minita; the Guatemalans stayed on the right side of the border. At least the Belizeans weren't weighed down by the worry of balance of payments deficits or terrorist bombings.

I asked Elizabeth across the reception counter: What was the most interesting thing to have happened recently? She looked confused, then consulted her friend. Both giggled, and Elizabeth said simply "Elections". They were obviously a source of some fun.

Elizabeth exuded contentment with her lot, a trait which seemed endemic amongst Belizeans. Why it would be so, I couldn't tell. There was so much that could be done with the country, yet it was only foreign conglomerates who wanted to exploit it. I was convinced the people should be doing something for themselves – even if it was just ripping off fat American tourists.

My mind conjured up dozens of schemes to turn Belize into a profit-making enterprise. Everything was here: natural resources, hot weather, plentiful labour. There was no good reason why someone with a spark of ambition shouldn't clean up here. I regretted not being a budding entrepreneur. Why didn't the Belizeans want the same?

During the journey along the Western Highway to the new capital of Belmopan I became increasingly wrapped in my daydreams. Like the logwood cutters who settled here two centuries earlier, I was convinced that here grew a fortune ripe for the harvesting.

I had hitched a lift with Sandy Davie, who was responsible for the small contingent from the Royal Air Force Regiment which guarded the international airport. He had been based in the country for some time, and took an intelligent interest in the people. Our talk was frequently interrupted as we struck the deep pot-holes which made a mockery of the road.

At one stage the road disappeared entirely. A bridge over a small creek had been washed away, and a temporary structure erected a short distance away. You had to be sharp to spot it, but Sandy was quick enough. I soon learned driving in Belize is a high-risk activity.

We threaded our way through the dusty, drab little settlements of Hattieville, Cotton Tree and Roaring Creek and into the new capital of Belmopan. The decision to move the seat of government fifty miles to the south-west of Belize City was taken nine years after it had been extensively damaged by Hurricane Hattie in 1961. Perhaps when Belmopan opened for government business in 1970, the few squat, concrete office buildings might have looked attractive. Since then the climate has taken its toll and they now resemble dirty brown shoe boxes.

As capital cities go, Belmopan has yet to prove itself a success. Ten years after its birth, the population was just over 3,700 – mostly civil servants. Yet the Government remains hopeful, as governments the world over tend to be. Something will always turn up.

It was still early, and we had the Land Rover all day. Why not see the Mennonite settlement at Spanish Lookout? Sandy had never seen it, and I had no idea what Mennonites were. Fossils, perhaps?

They were a religious sect, said Sandy, of Scandinavian or German origin. The Mennonites also kept themselves very much apart from the rest of Belize. A dusty gravel strip led off the Western Highway. The road was perfectly straight, broken only by the course of the Belize River. On either side the kind of rolling pasture which would be familiar to the farmers of Hampshire spread out as far as one could see. Instead of the palms and enormous ferns which abound elsewhere, the cattle grazed placidly amidst occasional clumps of pampas grass.

The Mennonites had somehow kept their fair hair and pale complexions, as well as their own language. They were aloof, apart. We stopped at a roadside shelter attached to a farm, and asked if we could buy food. As we ate, the children stared at us apprehensively. The atmosphere was not hostile, and yet I felt we were being unconsciously urged to leave.

The land and climate may have been tamed, but so had emotion and the joy of life. No-one laughed or smiled at us. The spark which fired Elizabeth and her friends had not caught alight in Spanish Lookout. Instead the Mennonites had introduced the cold, clinically efficient Western order I had wanted the Belizeans to introduce for themselves.

By the time we rejoined the Western Highway, the sun had started to go down. "It's the worst time to travel, you never know what you're going to hit," Sandy said. I remembered the missing bridge, and how he had noticed just in time it was not there. Would we have been so lucky in the dusk or at night?

Maybe the old Belize will not be so lucky. Change is being forced upon it, and the past will last only as long as Belize City's dying heart.

FABIAN ACKER

Haircut in Shanghai

Shanghai begins just outside the Jing Jang hotel. Inside, the Chinese culture is dominated by the presence of Westerners and cowed by the grandiose architecture of the hotel. Perhaps lost might be a better word. The hotel, which was apparently built by a homesick Berliner in about 1920, has rooms so large that guests often miss meals as they trudge round the bedrooms looking for a way out.

But with your back to the Jing Jang, you are face to face with Shanghai, once a cosmopolitan city but now reclaimed for China. True, the locals don't stroke your bare arm as they do in Tibet, to see whether it's covered in skin or a hairy sleeve. But one's presence in Department Store Number Four is still enough to make shop assistants giggle behind their hands, and children point you out to their parents and siblings.

The reaction in the barber's shop, compared with the department store, was far more intense but more suppressed. It was as if Enoch Powell had appeared at the Notting Hill Festival. Conversation stopped, as did scissors. Even the TV was ignored while I took the seat proffered to me by the disconcerted proprietor.

There was a sibilant exchange between him and a young lad I took to be Little Assistant Number Three.

"Why do I get all the lousy jobs?" I recognised the tone if not the words. "Look at that hair! It's thicker than a yak's coat! I'm going home."

"Another word out of you, Little Assistant Number Three, and you can go back to making pincushions. Go over and cut his hair. Cut it all off, for all I care, but do it! Now!"

Number Three shuffled over, and without actually meeting my eyes, gestured to ask me if I wanted – God forbid – to have my beard trimmed as well as my hair. I assured him that his responsibility stopped at my ears, indicated the desired length on my forefinger, and off we went. First two or three sheets of the *China Daily* were wedged around my collar, with many pauses while Number Three broke off to watch the TV. Then over to the basin, and with the protection of a polythene sheet he gave me a shampoo, distaste oozing from his fingertips.

When the ads were on the television he worked quickly, barely glancing up. This was reasonable, as in China the adverts are even more boring than the programmes, and in any case seem to be entirely devoted to toothpaste. But Number Three was obviously gripped by the story, and he maintained a stop–go progress until we got to the blow–dry.

By this time it was apparent that my hair wasn't diseased or dangerous; the scissors hadn't turned black and his fingers were still all there. He had begun to enjoy himself. He had cut a foreigner's hair, which was more than anyone else had done in this part of Shanghai, or even China. Who knows? – he might be ready to move into the shoes of Assistant Number Two.

He went over to the boss to discuss the styling requirements of a middle–aged Englishman. They came to a conclusion quite quickly; Mrs Thatcher had only recently visited China, and every patriot would want to emulate her. A bouffant style was the obvious choice.

The curious thing is that, despite the beard and brown hair, when he'd finished, I *looked* like Mrs Thatcher. I even felt like her, and decided against a tip; 90p was more than enough.

This summer only the old women were wearing the standard baggy blue jacket and trousers. The young women's wear was much more imaginative and based on illustrations from *Woman's Own* (circa 1920) with some embellishments culled from old Charlie Chaplin films. Footwear, for instance, consisted of cream or white wedge-heeled open-toed sandals. These were followed by calf-length men's socks with jazzy patterns up the sides. Flared tennis skirts were also *de rigueur,* although modesty was maintained by making them knee-length.

But it was in the T-shirts that the girls threw modesty to the wind. Traditionally, the Chinese bosom is well hidden, sometimes even suppressed, so as to give a nice flat even chest. But the girls this summer were wearing decorated T-shirts, drawing attention to these forbidden areas. And most of the shirts had the word "NANGHTY" written across in bold bright letters. Was this the name, I wondered, of Shanghai's heart-throb. Handsome, debonair young Nanghty, who had set new standards in Chicken Plucking Brigade '86?

The truth was even more bizarre. Whichever work brigade had made all those T-shirts that summer, just didn't know how to spell "naughty".

Men's dress, however, still clings to the traditional: in the summer, long blue shorts topped by a string vest, and perhaps calf-length socks above flip-flops. In winter, the blue uniform; at the ankles you can glimpse long-johns peeping out. Curiously, despite the ubiquitous presence of drying laundry – hung from the trees and from the windows and even strung between lamp posts – you'll never see any undergarments, men's or women's. A western observer might easily conclude that the Chinese don't wear any.

But, at least on the surface, men's fashions may be changing, just a year or so behind the women's. Some shops now have dummies in the windows, smiling broadly, dressed in smart new shiny suits, something like the manager of the Salford Odeon used to wear forty years ago.

If they were daring enough, the men could fit themselves out with a wide variety of different clothes. Over at Pei Luo Weng's shop, which, according to the guide book, "enjoys a good fame at home and abroad", they could buy suits of "any style and fit". They needn't be shy about knock-knees or even pigeon chests. The shop "is specially good at making well-fit suits for those with a peculiar build".

Just a stone's throw away is Zhonghua Men's Leather Shoes; the outstanding characteristic of its products is that "the uppers are tightly sown to the soles". And if this isn't enough to tempt the dowdy Shanghai male off the street, then he ought to know that "Queen Elizabeth of Britain once ordered 100 pairs of ladies shoes . . . for her daughter's wedding". Who, do you suppose, were the lucky recipients?

Surprising that she didn't order a few pounds of "cordyceps" at the same time. This is a herbal pick-me-up and "3 to 5 pieces, filled into a clean and chopped open duck's head" can cure a variety of ailments suffered by guests at banquets, such as "cough and gasp, and spontaneous perspiration". The guide book doesn't say how it is introduced into the body of the sufferer. One hopes it isn't by mouth.

Still, the symptoms are quite familiar; 3 to 5 pieces of cordyceps are just what one needs to ask for a haircut in Shanghai.

CLAIRE SEGAL

MEETING WITH BENIAMIN

All staring at my tights – a colour the fashion buffs call "petrol". Veiled hostility in eyes used to queuing for anything vaguely sheer and brown. Curiosity, suspicion, a whole line of silent faces. I try to keep counting, to pretend that the Metro map is intelligible to me despite the Cyrillic script. At the Hotel Sevastopol they'd said five stops to the Bolshoi. They'd even written the name of the station in "real" letters on a piece of lined, white paper, now rapidly becoming a scrunged-up, damp ball in my clammy hand. Stop; doors slide open. I walk along the beautifully marbled tunnels scarcely registering the tasteful Art Deco archways and chandeliers which had so impressed me only that morning. A hand on my shoulder; my heart leaps into my mouth. A middle-aged woman wanting to help check the name on my piece of paper. Smiles exchanged; her English is no better than my Russian.

I emerge into an unseasonally warm April evening. It's six o'clock but the sun is still shining brightly and I have begun to perspire into my petrol tights. "Meet next to the last pillar on the steps of the Bolshoi Theatre," he'd said on the phone; but I'd forgotten to ask whether he meant the last on the right or the last on the left. He'd be wearing a dark suit; but so were many of the youngish men. I had his picture, thanks to the "35" Pro-dissident group in London, but I'd left it in my hotel room in case someone asked me where I'd got it. The thought occurs to me that this is a ridiculously romantic moment – me standing on the steps of the Bolshoi waiting for a tall, dark stranger to appear . . .

All I'd wanted was to spend the eve of Passover with a Jewish family while on my eight-day school trip to Moscow and Leningrad. I'd told the other two teachers I was going off to meet some long-lost Jewish relatives – the less they knew, the better. I'd rung my husband in London just before leaving the hotel. They were just about to sit down to their service. I hoped I would be able to ring him later in the evening when I returned from mine.

"Shalom." Amazing how a cliché can actually work when the occa-

sion demands it. A brief handshake, a whispered exchange of names, then me running down the steps trying to keep up with the long legs of Beniamin Borgomolov. "No English," he warns me. No breath left for chatter anyway, as I half walk, half run in his footsteps.

Through a park, still denuded of greenery despite the early mild spell, past grey, concrete offices and small shops, down narrow side-streets into what must be the old part of the city. The houses begin to look crumbly and picturesque – French shutters and potted plants. My shoes are beginning to combine with my sweaty tights so that I'm walking half over my shoes to avoid the blisters. A half-hour's walk-run later my feet breathe a sigh of relief as we finally come to a halt in a public courtyard between some of the shuttered houses. Beniamin whispers that this is where we shall be meeting his wife, and that I still musn't speak. Meanwhile, passers-by stop to greet my obviously well-known companion and to cast curious glances in my direction.

By the time his wife and her friend arrive (from a Jane Fonda-type exercise class, of all places) Beniamin is palpably nervous. Two rather frumpily-dressed ladies of an indeterminate age greet me with the briefest of Shaloms and glance down at my tights. Into a taxi, half-an-hour's strained ride, then change to another taxi. Eventually we turn off the main road into the kind of sparsely-vegetated birch forests that always seem to play main characters in spy movies. By now we are at least an hour away from Moscow, in what looks like a country sub-urb, but without suburban houses. We draw up outside a concrete apartment block just like the ones I'd seen in the city. Again I'm warned not to speak as we walk up the stairs.

Inside the apartment I can finally speak in English, even though the friends of the Borgomolovs understand very little. Their flat (the first and last I was to see on my trip) reminded me ironically of the Ulpan flat I'd stayed in while visiting Israel – small, neat but slightly sordid in its meanness. And this couple are part of the "élite" – he an engineer, she an internationally-renowned surgeon. This is the first time, appa-rently, that Tania and Beniamin have not had the Seder service in their home – it is for the sake of the friend, who has never had the celebra-tion before and does not know how to go about it. His Russian wife (interesting how the Jews do not refer to themselves as "Russians"), is also interested in seeing how the ritual is performed.

The meal was set out on a small table in the room which served as both lounge and dining room. By Russian standards it really was a "feast" – soup, smoked fish, boiled potatoes, salads and eggs, and a kind of cake made from unleavened bread. I could well believe the women when they said they'd had to go to twelve different shops to get the food – I'd already had some personal experience of the notori-ous queuing system. The matzos were apparently a special treat – they'd been handed out in front of the foreign press at the Central

Synagogue in Moscow. The year before, Tania's father had been imprisoned for twelve months for making them. The wine, from Giorgia, was excellent. The special prayer-book for the occasion, translating Hebrew into Russian, had been brought in secretly by someone like myself.

Ironically it was I, with only a slight knowledge of the service and a patchy command of Hebrew, who had to come to Beniamin's aid in the running of the service. Few Jews, he informed me, now have the knowledge or skills to do so. And in spite of the simplicity of the fare, and the lack of expertise in the ritual, this re-telling of the striving for freedom of a small group in history had more significance for me then than at any time before or since.

After the meal they pressed me for details of my life in England and in Israel. They spoke openly of their frustrations – how Beniamin, the "most patient refusenik in the world", had been waiting nearly thirty years to join the rest of his family; how he'd lost his job as soon as he'd applied for his exit visa; how Tania had lost her university job when she'd tried; how the friend's wife had been refused permission to attend an international medical convention when the authorities found out that her husband was a Jew.

As I leave, the friends insist on pressing into my hands the few chocolates they have remaining. Outside it is a balmy evening and the journey back into the city is silent and uneventful. It is only after an emotional farewell to the Borgomolovs at the Central Railway Station, and after being placed in a taxi to take me back to my hotel, that I begin to relax. To my horror I notice a police-car flagging us down. The headline flashes through my mind: "Girl in Coloured Tights Imprisoned". My driver in deep discussion with the law, I try to think of a plausible excuse for being out alone in the middle of the night. Lots of head-nodding going on as I ponder my fate, until the notebook is flicked shut and my driver nonchalantly returns. Apparently nothing more than a minor traffic warning.

Past the Olga on duty on our floor of the Sevastopol and into the room which I share with Leletta. "How'd it go?" she asks, barely looking up from the novel she is reading on the bed. "Fine," I answer, "except for the ladder in my tights."

SUSAN KERR

GHIRLANDAIO'S CAT

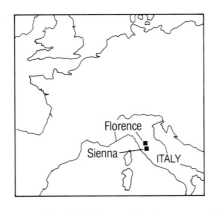

My shiatzu man said there's no point in being ill unless you learn something from it. So it was a philosophical bout with 'flu, and my elixir lay in watching clouds change shape. They merged with a year-long series of dreams – dreams of food, then flying, then aristocracy.

After the clouds came Tuscany.

I had expected to fall in love with its legendary landscape, and I did. But I had expected it to be cosy, like the English landscape, with its storybook hills and hedgerows. Instead, it is deeply satisfying: fertile, sensual, ripe, pleasing to the eye and soul. It is understandable that this land gave birth to the Renaissance. Undulating, varied, textured, Tuscany and adjacent Umbria have repeating rounded hills of bleached golden wheatfields, exclamation marks of cypress, small groups of olive trees, scarlet poppies, patches of vineyards, and four-square buff stucco houses with terracotta tile roofs.

With no towering peaks to dwindle the man, no boundless spaces to daunt the spirit, no comfortable valleys to suffocate vision, Tuscany is on an utterly human scale, the more so because its horizons call the dreamer. All around the rim of this golden world blue-upon-blue hills recede, layer upon layer, different blues each one. Gun-metal blue, lavender blue, fog blue, violet, slate blue, cigarette smoke blue, the blue of the Madonna's mantle. We are safely enclosed, but there is no telling where the mountains end and the sky begins. There is no limit.

In Florence I picked up a stray that has stayed with me ever since. I found it at the Convent of San Marco, while I was looking at Ghirlandaio's cool, gigantic fresco of the Last Supper. The usual participants are present; the beloved disciple has fallen asleep. Two of the Marys are there, too. Everyone is seated behind the table except Judas, who stands face to face with Jesus, locked in an eye-to-eye confrontation with the will of God. And there, on the black and white checkered tile floor, in front of the table, sits a piebald cat, looking out – at me. Everyone else looks within the picture, except this disturbing cat with amber eyes. It sits right of centre, accusing, challenging, or . . . questioning. Warning, perhaps. Examining? Testing? What is that extraordinary cat doing there?

What does a cat have to do with the Last Supper, or with the Italian Renaissance? I had to leave it behind as we went upstairs to the monks' cells to discover the frescoes of Fra Angelico, fresh as students' posters in a dormitory. Who could not dwell on the holy, alone with the exalted simplicity and the pure, unearthly light of the angelic brother's paintings? That they survived the fierce Savonarola's reign at San Marco surely is miraculous.

The cat came back to haunt me, appearing like the Cheshire Cat without a smile. It just looked with that look. And like the Cheshire Cat's smile, the look lingered.

Days later, many miles and frescoes later, on a morning that began with a "messe" in a thirteenth century church sainted with my own name, we went to Sienna. In the visual babble of the duomo, with its black-and-white banded columns densely packed as tree trunks in a redwood forest, as I stepped down after seeking and finding the myriad vistas through the columns, Ghirlandaio's cat pounced: the truth.

That is what it wants and why it wants me. The truth, the whole truth and nothing but the truth, "so help me God".

Later in the day, in the tall and narrow town of San Gimignano, which shimmers opalescent on its hilltop above the Tuscan fields, after we had seen the fresh, naive frescoes of its duomo – the creation of Adam by a six-seraph-enthroned God puffing visible breath, a pale placating Eve emerging by caesarian from sleeping Adam's side, the Renaissance Red Sea crossing, with the sea parted as clean as a comb parts hair – we came out to witness the Corpus Christi procession of prepubescent Tuscan girls radiant in First Communion white, their lined and weary mothers and grandmothers trailing after, followed by the wondrously tuneless brass band and canopied monstrance, and the straggle of husbands and fathers and brothers, through the one narrow street of San Gimignano, beneath the windows hung with red and golden banners as they've been hung for at least four hundred years of processions. We followed the scattering of rose petals back to the source of the procession, to the barn-like church of Saint Augustine, warm and reeking still of incense.

We gazed upon the story of the saint's life, clear and colourful as a child's colouring book: pink, green, overflowing, in the alcove behind the altar. We were the last and only visitors before the closing of the tranquil cloister. Only the sun, the shadows, the blue sky, the sound of bells to remind the past monks of the outside world. Then, in the extant family church, senses replete with frescoes, I was caught again by Ghirlandaio's unblinking cat: the truth or nothing else. The truth from now on or give up.

I often go back to Tuscany now. I climb into an iridescent bubble and I float. The bubble is glazed with the reflected blond of the fields, the red and pink and blue of the frescoes, brushed with gold leaf. I sit in my turquoise travel dress with my back against the curve inside the bubble, knees up, arms on knees. And I drift over the hills, east to Arezzo, to pink and white Assisi, to brave, grim Gubbio, north to Florence, west to sienna-coloured Sienna. I can see San Gimignano shining on its hilltop, and the golden saucer of landscape from the Pope's palace in Pienza, and the echoing square and that small Renaissance palazzo for sale in Montepulciano. And our own castle, Gargonza, with our view over the blue-distant Chiana plain.

In London I dream a new dream language, of different foods, and then of my garden, my new delight and passion. The garden calls me, with its pace of watching clouds and 'flu and floating over Tuscany in a bubble. It has the rhythm of truth. The plants, in my dream, are snug, with their earth blankets pulled up around their necks. They are still, but growing.

That cat of Ghirlandaio's is with me still, like the faithful dog of self-pity Alison Lurie invented. Only it isn't an eager dog pleading to get in, it's an independent cat who wants me on its terms. It won't come in when invited, but prowls, and disappears for days at a time, returning unexpectedly, demanding, with that look. Once or twice I have found it purring on my lap. But it will not stay and it also will not go entirely away.

HELEN BLACKMORE

HOLE IN THE SAND

It is just an ordinary hole, as holes go. Dug in the sand. About six feet by eight feet. Fairly shallow. Just deep enough for four bodies. The beaches of the Côte d'Atlantique, west of Bordeaux, are pock-marked with similar holes.

Occasionally a black Mirage fighter streaks low across the blue sky. A reminder of other times, other beaches, when men crouched, helpless, among the dunes and craters. But these French pilots are probably on the look-out for nothing more sinister than well-oiled, succulent, brown breasts. And the only threat from the Germans comes when, naked and ruthless in pursuit of their volley-ball, they bound over your hole, spraying their recumbent fellow-holiday-makers with sand.

There was a time when naturists and sun-lovers were confined to securely-fenced anthropological straw villages amongst the sand dunes, but now they frolic the length of the coast. ("For goodness sake! Take your swimming trunks *off,*" you whisper, embarrassed, to your eight-year-old. "I don't care what the boys say at school. Bums aren't rude!") But, however powerful the sun, a malevolent wind off the Atlantic can chill the naked body to a pattern of goose pimples or flagellate it with a whirl of sand. And so, calling upon an instinct almost eradicated by mortgages, dry rot, loft-insulation and damp-proof courses, urban man digs his private sun-trap in the sand.

Of course, nothing much happens when you spend your entire holi-day in a hole in the sand. Afterwards you have no entertaining travel-lers' tales of man-eating elephants or cracking ice floes. You cannot claim to have been winched to safety by a helicopter or marched away at gunpoint by freedom fighters. But you do discover that quite ordi-nary people take on a surreal quality when nude among strangers.

Look at those three retired stockbrokers paddling ankle-deep in the lace-patterned shallows of exhausted breakers. Modesty has obvi-ously driven them to a joint investment in a single outfit. One wears the jaunty red-and-white striped T-shirt, one the denim shorts and the third the straw boater. The heat shimmers, and for a moment tricks you with a glimpse of three curly-haired Edwardian boys with shrimping nets. But then you see the wrinkled necks, the self-satisfied bellies, the shrivelled scrota and the spindly legs. More like indolent, basking reptiles.

And what about that mountainous woman? Did you ever see the American Circus? The drums roll, the Ringmaster pronounces, the trumpets bray and the butch Fraulein Heidi stampedes through the curtains. Muscles rippling, she lifts her dainty white- and silver-clad companion in one hand and places her in a sparkling globe which she rotates, nonchalantly, on her nose, to thunderous applause. That woman, over there, picking sand from her nipples, she'd be transformed by Fraulein Heidi's spangled costume.

"Glâces! Boissons!" Alas, fame and glory escape her as the ice cream vendor, discreet in black swimming trunks, distracts her with a quid's-worth of ice-cream to share with her drooling, sand-clogged Scottie.

The portion of sea deemed "safe" for bathing and surfing is marked by blue flags and an umpire's chair. Does the immaculately-white-clad, handsome-but-unintelligent umpire decide whether each death by drowning was fair play? He watches black frogmen emerge from the sea; soon they will haul in their golden treasure chests, spraying the worm-bubbling sand with ingots and ducats. Ah! It's only surfboards they're groping for. They are just the unchic relatives of those lemon, turquoise and sugar pink rubber-clad surfing super-heroes; those men who crouch, crest, lurch, then swirl in with the spent breakers and scrabble ignominiously at your feet.

Meanwhile the children have found their second jellyfish. "Is it still alive?" they ask hopefully. You stare at the beached, transparent mound. "Well, I'm sure it's dead," you lie, remembering childhood stories of idyllic summers, invading Portuguese Men-of-War and infants killed by these floating plastic bags; "but perhaps we won't swim today." The protests start. "How about beachcombing? A bit further from the sea? In the dunes perhaps. See who can find the most unusual bit of metal or wood." An hour later, you realise you could start your own scrap metal business from the debris in the dunes.

All afternoon an old man with the face of Picasso stands on the dunes, hands behind his back, staring out to sea. He's still there as the sun sets spectacularly and you come panting back. Just standing by the rubbish bin. Staring profoundly at the sea. *"Pardon!"* you mutter, throwing Nivea bottles, apple cores, punctured balls and Camembert boxes wildly out of the bin over his feet. His gaze shifts as you locate a stained Sainsbury's bag. His wise blue eyes fixed on you, he discourses on art, philosophy and death. Or could he be inquiring how your car keys came to be at the bottom of the bin, covered with sticky melon seeds?

Car keys? Well, of course, no realist these days actually *sleeps* in the hole in the sand. At a safe distance of twenty minutes is the car and the family tent, surrounded by pine trees, several hundred other cars and tents, and all the trappings (including toilets that don't even smell French) of a 3-star Municipal Campsite. At the campsite you leave behind the flights-of-fancy of the beach. Here everyone is modestly dressed and cautiously behaved – even the family poodles. French social etiquette is best observed in the areas assigned for washing-up. The brow-beaten small man with two bowls of crockery (plates for first course, dinner-plates, side plates, salad bowls, fruit dishes, wine-glasses, coffee cups, pans, and extensive cutlery to match) might well commence a conversation with an attractive young woman, "Yours, I believe, is the charming dog three tents from ours?" They will be engrossed in details of the sleeping patterns and nocturnal walks demanded by their respective dogs, before his wife comes to reclaim him.

And beyond the campsite lies a small town. It looks like a cardboard model in lemon and pale blue, which can be folded flat and stored during the visitor-less winter months. The pharmacy is the most prosperous establishment, filled with exotic gilded perfumes and expensively packaged remedies for all ailments. The rest of the town comes to life when the market arrives. Traders ply you with their wares. You sip almond cognacs and taste the cheeses, Basque cakes, Vietnamese crisps and the pancakes, whilst declining to buy the amazing (look no butter!) pancake-pan.

Between the stalls of Indian and African fabrics you glimpse the bread, vegetables, fish and exotic cardigans. You perch on a stool at one of the busiest stalls and take a light lunch of champagne and local oysters.

But too much jostling can be fatiguing. You gather up the buckets and spades and head once more for the beach. You excavate two sand boats along the high-tide line from which the children can defy the incoming waves, then glance towards the dunes to check that Picasso is still meditating on the transcendence of the Atlantic. Reassured, you sink happily into your familiar hole, apply the ritual lotions and creams, place the token paperback on your stomach and stare vacantly at the blue sky, oblivious of all except the occasional roaring, swooping Mirage, mis-hit volleyball or hopeful shout of *"Glâces! Boissons!"*

DOWN THE INDUS

Climbing over the Zoji-la pass in a decrepit Kashmiri bus was like leaving India. No boundary could be better defined. In the long pull to the top the eye is soothed by the luxuriant, alpine vegetation of Kashmir, copybook green in the thin mountain air, and scalded by the brilliance of reflected light shimmering off the desert as the bus rolls into Ladakh. It is strange that in this impoverished landscape poverty does not have the same directness as in other parts of India. As a rebellion against the ever-encroaching desert, the Ladakhis assert their enjoyment with colour, with music and dance, in a burst of creative energy. Suddenly brown specks that seemed merely boulders in the landscape focus into children gaudily dressed in their little red coats and yellow headdresses heavy with gold, silver, amber and turquoise, waving the bus along with fiercesome joy.

"You know they only do that because the Indian soldiers throw their lunches to them."

My companion has an air of resignation from too much time spent in the East with too little enjoyment. But nothing can stop my excitement. Ladakh is an oasis of Tibetan culture cut off from India by its Buddhist tranquillity and the awesome barrier of the Himalayas.

The eye, bewildered by the labyrinth of different shapes, textures and shades, hesitates where to begin in this wasteland. The light continually shifts, giving the parched land a life of its own. One moment the mountains seem to crowd in ominously on the bus as it heaves its way over the passes; the next they open out into a vast expanse of emptiness, gold melts into the brilliance of blue and the silence where they meet is total.

In Leh all the traffic has come to a standstill. Not only does the cow refuse to be moved from her comfortable spot in the middle of the road, but all the traders' wares cannot be contained on the pavement and spill out in a tide of colour – apricots and amber, maize and gold. Then there are the shoppers who come with their yaks, donkeys, horses and mules adding mayhem to confusion. Not that it really matters, for there is too little vehicular traffic; but the congestion does become hazardous when a religious fanatic appears so absorbed in his devotions that he clobbers passers-by with his prayer-wheel.

Evening, and the traders are packing up. Young girls sway under their heavy loads and the after-effects of *chang,* the local barley beer. Old women in their wide, pointed, *perac* hats encrusted with precious stones, try to conduct an intimate conversation without prodding each others' eyes out. In the stillness of evening the smell hits me, probing my nostrils with the acrid scent of cow dung, yak butter, rotting vegetables and stale sweat. As the young boys, congregating around the cinema, become silhouetted against the night sky, the sound of rhythmic chanting echoes along the mountains.

"Om mani padme hum. Om mani padme hum." (Praise to the jewel in the Lotus crown, the sacred mantra of Avolokieshvara, the Budhisarva of Compassion.) The prayer follows me everywhere. Even in the silence of the desert the words are found written on a stray stone or sung in the wind by a solitary prayer-flag.

Throughout the summer, the road to Leh is busy with convoys of army trucks bringing supplies for the winter and gaudy, Kashmiri lorries that would look more at home in a circus than transporting goods to sell to the summer tourists. They breed dissatisfaction. Despite the smiles, despite the tranquillity, there is an atmosphere of wanting. The Ladakhi who runs my hotel is angry that his land is governed by Kashmiris.

"Ladakh is part of Jammu and Kashmir state, but it is culturally totally different from their Moslem society."

The pretty young girl who works in the Dreamland restaurant wants a jewellery shop she cannot have because too many Kashmiris monopolise the summer tourists. She tells me all this with a smile of contented resignation. Aggression does not exist in her vocabulary so she is patient. The Tibetan who runs the restaurant wants a country he cannot have. The plaintive demands "Hello bonbon", "Hello one pen", follow me around like a persistent echo. The children have learnt the merits of begging. It is an inevitable result of letting a trickle of the West down the Indus.

"No pen, no bonbon."

The children do not resent it. They take my hands.

"We three friends?"

We walk down the hillside. They are as nimble and surefooted as gazelles while I am outsized and tentative. Their voices rise in the glottal, tortured sound of song, while they play with my hat and scarf.

"Hello one pen."

"No pen."

They giggle, playing the foreigner opposite my Ladakhi. Begging has not yet become a serious occupation. It is an amusing hobby to be undertaken in the spirit of a joke – the children could just as easily turn the joke on themselves.

"What can I do?" The doctor was embarrassed to show me his consulting room. "I have so few facilities, and the people do not use the treatment correctly because they cannot communicate with the Indian doctors. However, there has been improvement recently. We have a new hospital near Leh and I am one of the first Ladakhi doctors."

I look at his little room with its medieval equipment and confectioner's medicine. Perhaps it is just as well to have such inadequacy, for it forces the people back to their faith. Every aspect of life is guided by religious rituals. But the magic of spirits and demons can survive only in isolation. Already their erosion has started.

"There are fewer boys wanting to join us," a monk at Thikse revealed. "The young men find a new method of escape on the road along the Indus to Srinagar instead of through the thought chambers of the mind. The lure of the West is stronger than their desire for enlightenment. I am sad not for myself, but for what others are missing."

The timelessness of Ladakh has been ejected into the supersonic present, where the cinema sits under the eye of the monastery, the plumbing exists side by side with the open sewer, and Toyota meets yak in the street.

"Please miss . . . miss . . . miss."

I am beckoned by the first of a new generation of language enthusiasts. Her family smile, relaxing in the stillness of the valley while the apricot trees glow in the twilight and the sky turns from pale pink to orange. The mountains soak up the last rays of sunshine and the valley shrinks into darkness. With the generosity of friends, they invite me to participate in their evening meal.

"Libya denies responsibility for the bombing attacks on . . . Liverpool City Council have decided to strike . . ."

They smile, eating *tsampa* and drinking *chang,* laughing at the noise from their new radio. I resent its penetration of these unspoilt valleys but I feel selfish in doing so. They do not want, nor are they able, to live in isolation any longer. They want better roads, better education, better facilities just as much as anyone. I am afraid because they do not understand the change and, therefore, may not be able to control it.

The road down the Indus from Srinagar to Leh is only 434 kilometres long, yet the two towns are separated by a vast chasm of time. How long before Leh joins Srinagar in consumerist frenzy? Or perhaps the Indian Army will finally decide that they want no more traffic down the hazardous road along the Indus, only five kilometres south of the Pakistan border, to a land that has large areas of disputed territory with China. Then the irony that such a peace-loving community should be at the centre of international politics and aggression will save Ladakh.

PAUL HARVEY

THE VOICE OF REASON

One of the photographs Magosha sent me from the previous year's visit (part of her campaign to make sure I didn't back out of The Plan) was of Darek, standing in the doorway of the guesthouse kitchen, holding a massive carving knife with which he was about to open a catering-sized can of sardines. He was grinning and wearing a black "Anarchy in the UK" T-shirt. In the autumn of 1985 Darek was nineteen, a chef from Gdansk, an expert on New Wave music who spoke an English learnt almost exclusively from bootleg tapes, graffiti, and the kind of imported pop magazines heavily frowned on by the authorities. He would appear occasionally from the smoky depths of the kitchen and offer me a bottle of the best Gdansk beer, obtained somehow from the supplies of the local military base. Despite such contacts, Darek was not a supporter of what is often in Poland called "The Regime".

"Fuck socialism," he announced one evening when we were sitting drinking beer and listening to his collection of Joy Division tapes. He shook his head in disgust: "Rebel youth is important! Positive Vibrations!" He opened another bottle: "You like Manchester bands?"

Magosha's idea of a reunion in Hel was hatched one vodka-soaked September evening down on the Baltic beach. She brushed aside any possible indecisiveness or objections with a mocking threat: "We mean it – we expect you." And so, surprisingly, twelve months and a few letters later, The Plan somehow came alive. Magosha and her sister Basha hitch-hiked from the northern port of Gdynia; Jacek and Janusz escaped from their duties in the Academy of Sciences Research Institute and squeezed themselves into a tiny Fiat 126 for the seven-hour drive from Warsaw; and, after two weeks in Gdansk, I left the university and caught the train to Hel, a slow meandering ride through the flat empty countryside, brushing the edge of the sandy northern plain where Poland tilts slightly downwards and drains into the Baltic. It drizzled most of the way and the train was full of soldiers. I spent the journey crushed up against a rain-streaked window wondering whether I was doing the right thing.

We all met up in Jurata, the last station on the peninsula before Hel, a small narrow holiday village surrounded by pine trees, with a road, a single-track railway and two coastlines ten minutes' walk apart. The Post Office had closed down at the end of the season but the fish stall was still doing good business with the few remaining visitors, and there was beer in the shop, temporarily at least. The rotting pier that Janusz had almost fallen through in the dark had survived another winter. The only thing missing – a year on – was Darek, who had been fired from his job and gone back to Gdansk. I looked at the cassette of The Screaming Blue Messiahs (Side 2: The Best of Serious Drinking) that I'd thought he might like and put it back in my bag.

The Hel Peninsula – a long, skinny sand-spit arm dividing part of the Bay of Gdansk from the Baltic – has a history containing the traditional Polish elements of power, invasion and enforced compromise. Reaching out more than thirty miles south-east from the north coast, strategically positioned for both fishing and conquest, it was the site of numerous naval battles against the Swedes in the seventeenth century and one of the last garrisons to be defeated by the advancing German troops at the end of the September campaign in 1939. It is so narrow in parts that resistance workers managed to dig sections of it into islands to annoy the Germans. Today it is back in one piece but its dual role is maintained in a mixture of fishing villages, holidaymakers and the inevitable military establishments.

I went back to Hel with the cold voice of reason whispering inside my head that you should never trust return visits. Telling it to be quiet only made it repeat, petulantly, that experience teaches you to beware of journeys undertaken for romantic reasons. It had a point, I knew: Reason always does. But then Hel *is* in Poland, a country where such voices, cold or otherwise, are given a hard time, and I did have what I considered to be another, very good reason for the Hel reunion, a reason I finally tracked down in the TV lounge of a seedy hotel, watching a badly-dubbed episode of *Return to Eden*.

"You're mad!" barked the Cold Voice Of Reason. "You'll regret it."

"Very probably," I muttered, trying to shut it out of my head. "Go away and leave me alone."

Iwona was wearing the same hairslide and didn't seem in the least surprised to see me.

We stayed there in the Hotel O'Limp (God knows where the name came from: Magosha, who knows about such things, claimed it was something to do with the Irish Catholic Society) swatting mosquitoes and listening to the anguished howls of the plumbing. Iwona had a job as a waitress, filling in a few months before moving back to Gdansk, her home town. Apart from mealtimes when she spent more time bringing us things than the manager thought reasonable, the six of us, with nothing to do except re-play some of the previous year's good times, wandered through the pine forests eating smoked eel and laughing at the groups of slimmers from a local private health club panting their way through the sand in a wobbling crocodile. When we went swimming in the freezing water the Voice Of Reason refused to join in and sat on the shore mumbling health warnings. The families of wild boar, tamed by tourist scraps, were still roaming the woods, all on an exact scale from large to tiny as though they might somehow fit one inside the other, like Chinese ivory figures.

As a foreigner who wasn't even registered with the police my only legal route down the Hel Peninsula was by train. The road ran through the middle of the same camp from where Darek had somehow smuggled the beer, and there were checkpoints on the road. "It's all highly secret," Jacek told me in a serious tone. "They're idiots, you get a much better view from the train." When the shop ran out of beer Janusz nearly got us arrested by standing outside the Party's summer retreat and shouting "Bolshevik brothel!" in Polish, after the hard-faced receptionist had refused to sell him any.

Out on the tennis courts and around the swimming pool, staunch supporters of "The Regime" stared from behind a wire fence. In a nearby restaurant the waiter explained that we could have anything we wanted as long as it was tea, because coffee was unavailable and the price of alcoholic drinks was rumoured to be about to rise by fifteen per cent, but no-one was sure when it would be. The VOR sneered quietly in my ear while Iwona gazed at the waiter for a while until he changed his mind and produced a dusty bottle of red wine. I'd probably have done the same.

That evening I locked the VOR in its room and we lit an illegal fire on the shores of the Bay of Gdansk, watching the pink September sun set in a blaze of pale northern light. Half a mile away, on the other side of the peninsula, the Baltic was grey and rough, autumnal undertows swirling their way along the edge of the shore, nibbling at the sand dunes. Was it here, I wondered, that the Resistance had done some digging? Perhaps Jurata *had* once been an island. It was certainly beginning to feel like one. We walked along the beach in the middle of the night, drinking vodka and listening to the sound of the surf breaking, counting stars and watching the lights of the ships in the distance. Janusz told us endless jokes about swimming to Sweden. At three o'clock in the morning Iwona smuggled us all back in and then raided the kitchen, producing bread, and sardines in a tin which she opened with a huge knife that looked somehow familiar. Next day the manager gave me an early-morning look and complained about the sandy footsteps on the stairs.

While Magosha and the others practised their English on me, Iwona tried to improve my Polish. She made me practise at mealtimes:

"Have you finished with the herrings?" "Could you pass me the beet-root soup?", brushing my arm lightly with her sleeve as she moved around the tables under the disapproving stare of the manager. When the sun shone we lay on the sand under the pine trees, a ridiculous combination of romance and Slavonic phonetics. The VOR refused to learn any Polish, which was a good excuse not to talk to it.

But the more the language began to make sense, the less I felt I really knew about Poland. There – stuck out on the road to Hel – nobody bothered asking me (as they'd constantly done when I was an official visitor) why I'd come to Poland and what my reasons were for want-ing to return to such a depressing, hopeless, ruined country. As far as I knew, the only "observer" was the Cold Voice Of Reason and by now we'd almost stopped communicating. But then the other side of Poland is that you never really do know what is happening. As an out-sider the system looks like a chilling form of half-organised madness but it appears too incomprehensible, too crazy, too sad for it to have happened accidentally: you begin to think, following Reason's logical arguments, that it must have been *planned* that way by those who want or need it to be like that. That the downward spiral of shortages, in-efficiencies, lies and paranoia are part of somebody's grand scheme to bring Poland to her knees. Who knows? Maybe they are. Even miles away from the grey urban monotony there are images of a Poland lost in someone else's power game: men in ill-fitting shabby suits drunk on the streets; women with headscarves staring expressionlessly from park benches. If you stopped to think about it too much it would make you cry. The more you discover, the less you understand. At the back of my mind the Cold Voice of Reason nodded wisely: "I told you so," it said, and then vanished.

On a damp grey late-September morning Basha and Magosha caught an early train out of Jurata. Basha had a chance – a faint chance – of a computer job with a firm in Copenhagen. Magosha went back to her job cutting up rats in a Warsaw laboratory. We agreed that The Plan had been a success and promised to write to each other. I stayed on for a couple of days partly because of Iwona and partly to teach Reason a lesson.

When Iwona and the manager finally fell out and she decided to go back to Gdansk to look for another job, I went with her as far as the air-port. She told me she had an idea where she might be able to find Darek, so I gave her the Serious Drinking cassette and asked her to re-mind him about the need for Positive Vibrations. She was still wearing the same hairslide when I kissed her goodbye.

At Warsaw Airport I bought a bottle of vodka for $1.80 and had an argument with the Voice Of Reason about Another Possible Plan. Goodbye is one of the easier things to say in Polish, but then that's only the pronunciation.

CAROLINE WHITE

It Takes Two

Seventeen floors up the wind jives around the tower blocks. The shriek and peal of car horns, burglar alarms, whooping police sirens, and laughter and shouting ricochet back and forth, caught by the wind and flung against the walls until the early morning. From the front window of the apartment, the buffeted blocks jostle for space and frame the view, a tiny triangle in the corner showing the lake frothing and foaming, speed and pleasure boats looping across its surface. The back window, where the spiders have made their homes, provided a box seat for myriad window scenes in the block across the street, televisions flickering backstage; and into the distance flash the fairy lights of a ubiquitous Walgreens next to a vacant parking lot, and where one of the many false façades – a church complete with stain glass and portals – adorns the side of another condominium, which itself dwarfs the Rumpelstiltskin houses beside it. The city is too small to escape in, too large to take refuge.

It's summer in Chicago and the run-up to Labor Day weekend: the heat and the noise pound the streets. The Pooper Scoopers are working overtime, and in the centre of the city restaurants spill out on to the sidewalks – except, that is, the singles bars, where long queues trail around the block joining Division and State, where seekers "hit on" each other behind the smoked glass and Budweiser. For those who prefer the more public chase, a wider choice and, inevitably, better lighting, there's the beach. If you're staying in the city over the Labor Day weekend, the beach is the closest to a holiday, even if four lanes of traffic from Lake Shore Drive career noisily right beside it and the award-winning, lunging shadows of the lakeshore skyline, twisting, curving, and glittering their way into the cobalt beyond, loom across unwary dozers by mid-afternoon.

On the low wall of the sidewalk promenade sprawl amateur film crews, focusing their zoom lenses on the scantily clad. The scantily clad, meanwhile, look on expectantly or stare pointedly; and in the movement of the single towels across the sand, like afternoon chess, there is still a semblance of surprise and coyness: "You alone?" "Great

book, I just read it." By five o'clock the lucky ones will have made
dates and the disappointed will be left to scan the classified in *The
Reader:* "Singles with graduate level education – Evanston", "Big
dances, all singles invited – Arlington Heights", "Advanced degrees
introductions – $12.00 includes drinks, hor d'oeuvres, dancing", "The
singles express welcomes all singles over 25 to a dynamite evening".
The invitations fill columns and take in every creed and status. And if
the prospect of the real thing seems a little too much, phone sex is
available – major credit cards accepted, and charge accounts opened
immediately. But wait, under the What's On, for one day only, is
another enticement – from 7 to 10pm at the Lincoln Park Market, a
chance to do the late night shop for groceries and love is for the taking.

By seven-thirty two television network film crews have assembled
outside the store. They drive foot-long microphones under the chins
of the shy, the bold, the curious and the totally bewildered. But this
was the wrong moment to ask questions. Customers and would-be
lovers were reticent – "I always shop here", or "I'm married" comprised the extent of the confessions. Undeterred, the film crew barged
in through the bottle-neck where two other similar crews were already playing chase down the aisles to the blasting rhythms of
Madonna, The Archies and The Supremes. A compère announced a
string of prizes, candlelit dinners for two, and details of the dancing
competition. A panel of female assistants attended to the business of
slapping self-adhesive name tags to their respective owners, loudly
advising in the process. "That means you're single and you're
dangerous."

A human bear advertising beer tried hard to hug whomsoever
strayed too close, but why bother with beer when champagne was
being given away two aisles along? A few bewildered shoppers tee-
tered nervously by the entrance, shopping baskets slung over their
arms, and one or two were valiantly fighting their way through the
give-aways of chocolate fudge cherry cola, nachos and chilli, cheese,
pizza portions and cookies. The assistants at the tills, trapped inside
their cash register podiums, looked on glumly at the advancing tide of
dancers and diners, squeezing past the meat and dairy produce to the
frozen foods, where the pace was a little quieter and afforded protection from the compère's marauding entreaties to dance and be bold.
By eight-thirty the limbo dancing had begun, with the aid of a broom
strung between the salads and the canned fruits. The assistant store
manager was dancing on top of the available counter space, and the
photographer hired by *Singles Magazine* was gathering a gallery of
action shots. The champagne salesman enthused wildly, "It's a great
way to introduce new products to a very upscale group of people.
You're gonna see a big increase in sales, a very big increase in sales".
The representatives from Jazzercise and *Marketing Magazine* echoed

every sentiment, commenting that this was a soft sell and by far the best way to sell.

The softly sold, meanwhile, had dispensed with their initial caution and were openly enjoying the chase: one remarked that he was very sorry that he had already eaten dinner before coming to the store as he could have had a free meal: another that the only places to meet people were bars and churches; another that at twenty-six she realised that she now had only a fifty per cent chance of getting married. A nattily dressed man in charcoal and red had finally plucked up the courage to ask a woman to dance, and the store manager revealed how many people come back and tell him that they got married as a direct result of meeting in the store while shopping. If reports conflicted as to which side of the States this idea had originated, no-one seemed to care: three thousand people had tried their luck, two hundred bottles of champagne had been drunk, and the manager was all set to try out the idea again, perhaps in a month's time.

The following morning, one of the choices on the radio dial was a telephone dating service. Two women searching for love had come into the studio and after talking about themselves and their requirements, serious male callers were invited to phone in with as articulate a description of their physique and personalities as possible. The women joked and flirted, and egged on by the presenter, finally made their choices. The early morning television news carried a report on the worrying fact that over a third of the population of Chicago were single. Outside, the wind still blew around the towers and the beauty parlour advertised the benefits of its 24-hour service.